Stop Watering Dead Plants

Stop Watering Dead Plants

Norm Sawyer

Norm Sawyer

Cover Art: Kane Sawyer
Photos: Norm Sawyer
Cover Graphics: Lee MacLennan

Published by

First Page Solutions
Kelowna, BC, Canada

DEDICATION

To all my readers who want to understand.

CONTENTS

Foreword... 1
Drowning... 2
Part One: Stop Watering Dead Plants...... 4
Stop Watering Dead Plants....................... 6
Whose Eugenics....................................... 11
Bitter Root... 16
Situational Depression............................. 20
Worse Than Dead..................................... 26
What Is Your Cheat?................................. 30
Sore Losers.. 34
Mockers And Scoffers.............................. 38
Conditioned For Cruelty........................... 43
Stumbling Blocks..................................... 49
Part 1: Questions for Understanding........ 54
Part Two: Perspective.............................. 56
Perspective.. 58
A-I And I... 62
We Can Spin It!... 67
Tribalism... 71
You Can't Go Back................................... 76
A Real Trust.. 81
Confidence Of Heart................................ 86
The Peter Moment................................... 90

I'm The Wrong Fisherman...................... 94
Part Two: Questions for Understanding.. 99
Part Three: Try Again........................... 100
Lock Stock And Barrel.......................... 102
Then They Were Gone.......................... 106
Why?... 110
Broken? Fix It!..................................... 114
Time To Dream Again........................... 118
Huummmmmmmmmmmmm................... 122
Seriously?.. 126
God Also Loves Atheists....................... 130
One Way Ticket.................................... 135
Our Dishonorable Honorables................ 138
The Junk Drawer.................................. 142
Am I Relevant?..................................... 146
If Not Now, When?.............................. 151
Part Three: Questions for
Understanding...................................... 156
Part Four: Timeless Principles................ 158
Richly Blessed...................................... 160
The Word Can Heal Or Sting................ 164
An Encouraging Word........................... 168
Double-Talk... 173
What Can God Do?.............................. 178
Keep The Windows Open...................... 182
The Fool And His Folly......................... 187

The Disciplined.. 191
Giving Away An Inheritance...................... 195
Life Moves On... 199
Part Four: Questions for Understanding.. 204
Part Five: Rest In Your Salvation.............. 206
Imitate Me... 208
I Am Contagious... 212
No Call-Waiting.. 216
Homecoming... 221
A Year In Review.. 225
All That May Be Desired............................ 230
Infinite And Eternal................................... 234
For Better Or Worse................................... 239
Even Faith Healers Die.............................. 243
Last Words... 247
Part Five: Questions for Understanding... 252
About the Author.. 253
Connect With Norm.................................... 254

FOREWORD

Wow! Norm, you've done it again! Another book! In Bible school Norm was my teacher and I often had the opportunity to be his "scribe". Today, he is publishing books one after another.

As you read Norm's new book "Stop Watering Dead Plants", you will soon realize that Norm is a straight-shooter, from the hip, no holding back. Norm shares real life situations and presents God's wisdom and solutions by weaving the word of God to set us free and to choose life and not death. If any offense is taken, focus on Jesus. Allow Him to massage your heart and plough through to victory. Let Go and Let God.

Thank you, Norm, for your inspiration. I recommend everyone order this book.

Doris Marciski

Norm Sawyer

DROWNING

The light in you was life for me
but having missed the fatal, ending cues,
in arid soil of unmet expectations-
I flooded with tears that you refused.
With hope and futile cultivation
watering in vain, thus overflowed
The withered desert of your heart
Hung dark for me, where I once glowed.
In peace, I sprinkled you with forgiveness,
fertile words, though unaware,
Poured over you, sparing hesitation,
Muddied reason without a care.
With every drop in vain, I sought
to ripen sweet on a barren vine,
I saw the light of what could be-
Depleting, consuming, and drowning
mine.

Jami Rogers

PART ONE:

STOP WATERING DEAD PLANTS

Stop Watering Dead Plants

Bemoaning the fact that you cannot get everything you want sounds like a sad drawn-out note that irritates everyone around you. Change your tune to the sound of the Lord's blessings and water what God has sown in your heart for His purpose. Phil. 2:12b Work out your own salvation with fear and trembling.

STOP WATERING DEAD PLANTS

Proverbs 11:25 The generous soul will be made rich, and he who waters will also be watered himself.

I understand that when people do not know God, they throw out a flare-prayer request to the powers that be, asking for success in their worldly endeavours. They are doing what they think a god is used for. I get it. We were all there at one time before we met God the Father, through Jesus Christ. We would kind of look up and say, "If you are real God, maybe you can do this for me or give me this thing." However, Christians ought to know better when asking by faith, what God's will is for their lives. Sometimes, Christians will ask God to bless something that has been long dead or has no resurrection life in it. They will also keep asking for a "Yes" on a dubious want when God has already said "No" to it.

Stop asking God to bless what is not blessable. Quit trying to twist God's arm into agreeing with your choices of sins and iniquities. This is what the non-saved do. Stop making the word of God say what you want to permit yourself to do outside of God's will. This is what immature Christians do. The Lord cannot agree with the sin you take pleasure in. Hab. 1:13a **But you are pure and cannot stand the sight of evil. Will you wink at their treachery?** How can a holy God bless our sinful choices? Stop watering dead requests. We need to align ourselves to the Lord's standard of living through Christ and not ask God to come down to our state of degradation. 2Cor. 6:17 **Therefore, come out from among unbelievers, and separate yourselves from them, says the LORD. Don't touch their filthy things, and I will welcome you.**

God cannot support our choice to disobey, and the Holy Spirit will always bring conviction within our souls when we are walking in disobedience. If a person has lost their peace, that is a good indication that God is not blessing their recent choices. The love of God for every person is never in doubt, but God's blessing upon our lives can wane because of our desire for a sinful lifestyle that leads to death. Plus, that sinful desire is not a joy to the Lord nor can He permit it. Why would we give our heart's love to dead projects and ways of living that God will not bless? Let the dead things die if they are not of God. Luke 9:60 **Jesus said to him, "Let the dead bury**

their own dead, but you go and preach the kingdom of God." We need to change our focus and take our eyes off what the Lord considers a dead issue, and refocus on the things that bring life to our souls.

It is only after the prodigal son had wasted everything he had, and participated in every kind of misspent activity that he finally woke up to himself. He realized that God was not blessing anything he did. From a rich heir to a low-level servant, dishing out pig slop that he was thinking of eating because he was starving. All because of his lifestyle choices. Luke 15:16 **He longed to fill his stomach with the pods that the pigs were eating, but no one gave him anything.** He had come to a place where no one gave him anything. I'm only speculating here, but what happened to all the people who helped him waste his inheritance? Where were the comrades and joyful pats on the back that came from the so-called friends who helped him sin his life away? The prodigal kept watering a dead lifestyle, and the lifestyle was giving him back the death he had sown.

Gal. 6:7 **Do not be deceived, God is not mocked; for whatever a man sows, that he will also reap.** The futility of watering dead plants is a

waste of water, and so do we waste our lives when
we follow a parallel path. If we sow death, then
death is the harvest we get. Someone might say, "I
thought the generous soul will be made rich. Why
did the prodigal son not get richer as he lavishly
spent everything on everyone? If that is how the
prodigal son blew his wealth, he learned the hard
lesson. Being a good steward of God's wealth,
and being irresponsible with - whatever money
can buy - are two different things. God gives us
wealth to be a blessing and an encouragement to
those who are trying to make it in life. We are
not to add to the cursed life that so many people
are living. Don't water the dead things of the
world that are at work in another person's life.
Help God's goodness water them so they can
get out of the dead zone they find themselves in.
Prov. 11:25 **The generous soul will be made
rich, and he who waters will also be watered
himself.**

I know people who keep watering terrible
family relationships that are dead and have been
dead for years. Some water dead friendships only
end up drained of life themselves because they
keep giving everything to the friendship. These
people are wasting water through their own
efforts, and they need to know that only prayer to
God for the family and friends' souls who have

become dead bones need God to do the watering with His life-giving waters. Rev. 22:17b **Let the one who is thirsty come. Let the one who desires take the water of life freely.** We are God's hand extended, but we are not God. Stop watering dead issues, and give that mess over to God. Only the Lord knows how to bring the dead back to life, so ask God to do the watering for you. Eze. 37:5 **This is what the Lord GOD says to these bones: I will cause breath to enter you, and you will live.** Amen and amen!

WHOSE EUGENICS

Proverbs 14:12 There is a way that seems right to a man, but its end is the way of death.

Eugenics: *The study of how to arrange reproduction within a human population to increase the occurrence of heritable characteristics regarded as desirable.* Humm, who are the ones determining what is regarded as desirable? Our history has had a few megalomaniacs who tried eugenising - if that is a word - a race of people that would coincide with their vision of human perfection. This ugly philosophy has a way of sneaking into the scientific community under the guise of wanting to enhance the betterment of mankind. It also has a way of leaking into political rhetoric to protect a certain segment of the population from the unwashed per se. However, as history demonstrates, human beings cannot be perfected outside of God's intervention.

The blood of Jesus has the power to change a soul to fulfil the requirements of God the Father's standard of righteousness regardless of who a person is. Eugenics, as practised among the monumental arrogance and the wilfully conceited, may at best, have a limited power to help develop a certain quality of perceived supremacy, (again, whoever determines what that is,) but, at the end of their efforts, they still have a human being in need of salvation. That person's soul will still require the cleansing power of the blood of Jesus to give him or her eternal life. This Frankensteinian approach that says we can create a flawless man is erroneous because it is a flawed man trying to do the creating. God says, "I am your creator." Psalm 100:3a **Know ye that the LORD he is God: it is He that hath made us, and not we ourselves.** Plainly said, "It is He who has made us, and NOT we ourselves."

The Lord's method of eugenics actually works for all mankind because our Heavenly Father is the original eugenicist. God, our creator, had no intention of leaving anyone out of His eternal plan, therefore, our Lord designed diversity within mankind. He also implemented what it would take to bring His plan to fruition. God takes the weak, sick, rich, poor, healthy, and every ethnicity there is and makes us the righteousness of God through Christ. I know this will bother all the pitifully boring supremacy groups, but there it is, we are one in Christ, regardless of race, colour, or ethnic background. Rev. 15:4b **All** nations will come and worship before you, for your righteous acts have been revealed. All nations, mean all nations. Even though mankind is constantly trying to eliminate a particular segment of the population they deem unworthy to live, God, in His love, still wants all nations to come and worship Him.

In the book of Esther, we read how Haman hated the Jews and plotted to destroy and remove them from the earth. Est. 3:8 **Then Haman approached King Xerxes and said, "There is a certain race of people scattered through all the provinces of your empire who keep themselves separate from everyone else. Their laws are different from those of any other people, and they refuse to obey the laws of the king. So it is not in the king's interest to let them live.** The more things change, the more they remain the same. These plots and ambitions are still desired by some nations today. We can't seem to run out of people to hate.

Haman felt inferior and lashed out to destroy the segment of the population that made him feel that way. Instead of improving and growing in character, he chose genocide as a solution. By eliminating a segment of the population, Haman felt it would enhance the standing of the people group he was part of, thus making them a superior race. Prov.14:12 **There is a way that seems right to a man, but its end is the way of death.** The plot backfired as so many of these plots do, and Haman ended up sentenced to hang on the gallows he had built for his hated enemies. Est. 7:10a **So they hanged Haman on the gallows that he had prepared for Mordecai.** Not only did Haman's prejudice get him killed, but the far-reaching stench of his ignorant philosophy also got his ten sons hung as well. Est. 9:13 **And Esther said, "If it please the king, let the Jews who are in Susa be allowed tomorrow also to do according to this day's edict. And let the ten sons of Haman be hanged on the gallows." 14 So the king commanded this to be done. A decree was issued in Susa, and the ten sons of Haman were hanged.**

The philosophies of eugenics and ethnic cleansing seem to run hand in hand and tend to support each ideology with the same evil intent. Eugenics says, "Let's breed perfection into the sub-human race," and ethnic cleansing says, "Let's kill the breed of sub-humans we don't approve of and remove them from our sight." Both concepts are anti-God, anti-Christ, and racist. Let us remember what Jesus said, "Whosoever believed in Him, shall not perish, but have eternal life." Whosoever is all nations. Be careful of the rhetoric you start high-fiving. You might be agreeing to terminate your own life and those you love. Most of the people reading this come from a people group who were once persecuted for just being alive. We were all made in the image of God. That ought to be acceptable. Amen!

Norm Sawyer

BITTER ROOT

Proverbs 14:10 The heart knows its own bitterness, and no outsider shares in its joy.

Dante said, "Heresy is a form of intellectual bitterness."

In Chapter six of the Gospel of John, Jesus had been expounding some very deep and profound teachings as to who He was. There came a point when the disciples would have to choose Jesus and accept Him as the God-given sacrifice to the world. Jesus was causing all His followers to make a choice to believe, or not believe, who He said He was. Many of the disciples were incredulous as to how Jesus described Himself because they were reasoning within their momentary thoughts and not by faith. John 6:60 **Therefore, when many of his disciples heard this, they said, "This teaching is hard. Who can accept it?" 61 Jesus, knowing in himself that his disciples were complaining about this, asked them, "Does this offend you?**

Jesus was asking them, "Is what I am saying causing you to become offended and bitter in your faith toward myself and God, who sent me?" John 6:66 **From that time many of his disciples went back, and walked no more with him.** The Lord had drawn a line of belief in the sand that would either bring out the faith in a man's heart toward God, or a root of bitterness exposing a faith lived out of convenience and personal interpretation.

The Lord asked His closest disciples if they would also leave Him, because of who He said He was, and the depth of relationship that would be required of them. John 6:67 **Then said Jesus unto the twelve, Will ye also go away?** Like Peter, we may ask ourselves, "Where can we go? God is God, and we don't have all the answers." John 6:68 **But Simon Peter answered Him, "Lord, to whom shall we go? You have the words of eternal life.**

Those who left in bitterness had to deal with the argument that was now aggressively clamoring in their hearts and minds. The peace that was once available to them because they had fellowship with Jesus, was now waning and the root of bitterness was sliding in. When bitterness finds its way into a heart, it is normally after a conflict of belief or disobedience toward God. If the person does not run to God to resolve the conflict of heart or repent of the sin of disobedience, then their heart is open to bitter thoughts and they are vulnerable to deception.

We know that Jesus taught anything but heresy. However, He was accused of heresy throughout His false trial. The intellectual reasoning that the religious leaders were using to rationalize their own heresy, was because they were looking for a saviour to deliver their physical lives from the oppression of Rome. Jesus was trying to deliver their souls from eternal death, and that would take faith in God's Son. Since the teachings of Jesus were contrary to the agendas of the religious leaders; in blind anger, they deemed it heresy. They wanted their interpretation of truth to justify their doctrines of nationalism. It did not matter how bitter of heart they became.

We who are in Christ, are invited by God to come to Him and find the grace needed to deal with the hard things we are going through. We may not get the answer we want to hear, but the Lord will meet the need of our heart and give us the courage to have faith in what God has said to be true. Heb. 4:16 **Let us therefore come boldly unto the throne of grace, that we may obtain mercy, and find grace to help in time of need.**

God does invite us to come and reason with Him, but the outcome of the reasoning is to clean our minds, hearts, and souls from sin and deception. God will welcome a contrite heart, but will work on cleaning up a bitter one. Isa. 1:18 **Come now, and let us reason together, saith the LORD: though your sins be as scarlet, they shall be as white as snow; though they be red like crimson, they shall be as wool.**

If you have found yourself in a bitter place, or have had a root of bitterness displaying itself through your thoughts, words, and actions - then it is time to draw closer to God. Let Him heal your inner man so that your outer man becomes the person God made you to be. The Lord did not save us to become bitter. God has something better for us. He saved us to give us a full and abundant life now, and forevermore. John 10:10b **I am come that they might have life, and that they might have it more abundantly.**

SITUATIONAL DEPRESSION

Proverbs 27:21 As the fining pot for silver, and the furnace for gold; so is a man to his praise.

I am not a doctor and do not understand the complexities of physical and mental depression. I do not have the training it takes to understand and diagnose chemical imbalances that some people suffer from and in turn the suffering manifestation of debilitating depression.

The depression I understand is situational depression that comes from unrepentant sin or carrying guilt and shame that has taken over someone's thought processes to the point of no longer caring for the things of God. Situational depression happens to everyone. The only difference with a lot of people who fall into this type of depression is that they get out of it by faith through the word of God and help from the Holy Spirit.

There are many who fall into this type of despair when they see the events that are taking place in the world. Many people feel like they are part of biblical prophecy and there is nothing they can do about it. Matt. 24:7 **For nation shall rise against nation, and kingdom against kingdom: and there shall be famines, and pestilences, and earthquakes, in divers places.**

These desperate people become overwhelmed by the circumstances of twenty-four-hour constant information overload of broadcasted bad news, causing a breakdown into depression. There are so many bad things going on and there is nothing that can be done about it. A feeling of hopelessness begins to move into the soul.

David was being hunted to death by King Saul and his army. David found it hard to keep himself high in spirits, yet he found the way to do it in spite of the circumstance he was in. Psalm 43:5 **Why art thou cast down, O my soul? and why art thou disquieted within me? hope in God: for I shall yet praise him, who is the health of my countenance, and my God.**

David was stating that the mood of his heart and the feelings of his soul was manifesting as depression; however, in the same verse David also comes up with the solution for the depression he was experiencing and that was to hope in God and start praising Him in the situation regardless of how he felt at the time.

Praising God is a way out of a desperate and depressive situation because God is in the very praises that start to come forth out of our hearts and only good can come out of anything God is involved with. Psalm 22:3 **But thou art holy, O thou that inhabits the praises of Israel.** God is in the praises of His people. God is in us and we are in Him. God is in the praises that the people He is in are saying, "Praise the Lord." In this case, praise will help diminish situational depression.

Another example is Elijah defeating Jezebel's prophets. 1Kings 19:1 **And Ahab told Jezebel all that Elijah had done, and withal how he had slain all the prophets with the sword.** However, after a great defeat over the false prophets Jezebel threatens Elijah with death. He ran for his life and in the same breath wants God to kill him. What happened to cause such a depression of fear? 1Kings 19:4 **But he himself went a day's journey into the wilderness, and came and sat down under a juniper tree: and he requested for himself that he might die; and said, It is enough; now, O LORD, take away my life; for I am not better than my fathers.**

He says, "I am no better than my fathers." Is that some sort of personal shame, because of the feeling of nonperformance? I think the problem was what happens to a lot of people in ministry. They start thinking they are all alone and there is no one else to do the work. They become overwhelmed with the call on their life, shamed into thinking they have failed. 1Kings 19:14 **And he said, I have been very jealous for the LORD God of hosts: because the children of Israel have forsaken thy covenant, thrown down thine altars, and slain thy prophets with the sword; and I, even I only, am left; and they seek my life, to take it away.** This is not true, of course, because God says to Elijah "There are seven thousand who have not knelt to Baal nor kissed him." God helps Elijah refocus on the message that was originally in his heart.

Jonah was going through a state of situational depression because he did not want the enemy of Israel forgiven. So he ran away from God, trying to force God's hand to judge Nineveh. Ah, the plans of mice and men. When the lot fell on Jonah during the storm at sea, Jonah said to the sailors to throw him overboard into the sea and the storm would stop. Jonah 1:15 **So they took up Jonah, and cast him forth into the sea: and the sea ceased from her raging.**

Jonah, after spending three days and three nights in the great fish that was prepared for him by God, begins to repent. Jonah 1:17 **Now the LORD had prepared a great fish to swallow up Jonah. And Jonah was in the belly of the**

fish three days and three nights. There comes a point where Jonah repents from his sin and the fish spews him out and Jonah is sent on the same mission to Nineveh. After Jonah ministers the word of the Lord in Nineveh the citizens repent.

God is pleased, but not Jonah. Jonah 4:2 **And he prayed unto the LORD, and said, I pray thee, O LORD, was not this my saying, when I was yet in my country? Therefore I fled before unto Tarshish: for I knew that thou art a gracious God, and merciful, slow to anger, and of great kindness, and repents thee of the evil.** Did Jonah ever get over his depression about his enemies receiving the same mercy that was available to Israel? I believe he did because of the fact that he records such a scathing account of his character during this time. Jonah is honest about himself and God; therefore because Jonah is able to be so truthful about himself speaks to his heart change in God.

What about you? Is there something you are carrying that could be dissipated with praises to God Almighty or repent of some nonsense that you are fed up with? Is there something of shame you have to let go of that has been eating away at your peace? These are all tricks of the enemy of our soul to keep us in a state of depression where there is no joy. I know the cure to this depression. It is Psalm 47:1 **O clap your hands, all ye people; shout unto God with the voice of triumph.** Psalm 150:6 **Let every thing that hath breath praise the LORD. Praise ye the LORD.**

WORSE THAN DEAD

Proverbs 2:18 For her house sinks down to death and her ways to the land of the departed spirits.

What can be worse than being dead? I think existing within an empty life, and not living the life God gave us could be as bad as being dead. Having no reason or purpose to get up, would be a terrible daily death. Always chasing the elusive - if I could have that, then I would feel alive, would be an empty existence, because the thing wished for is continually out of reach. I believe having to contend with the knowledge that we are wrapped within death's grasp and not able to do anything about it, could be frightening and weigh heavily on our soul. Being conscious of the fact that our bodies are in a state of dying, and heading to the end of life as we know it, can gnaw at our consciousness.

The reason we cannot phantom not existing is that there is a deep knowing in our soul that we will live forever. In most cases, this feeling cannot be explained, but there is an intuitive knowledge concerning its reality. Eccl. 3:11b **He has planted**

eternity in the human heart, but even so, people cannot see the whole scope of God's work from beginning to end. We know that we know, we will live forever, but in what state of being, we do not know. To think about the idea of being eternally dead, yet living in that state is a hard concept to process. Therefore, these introspections are pushed to the side hoping the mental anxiety these thoughts cause goes away.

Some people choose a dead life and are keen on causing others to do the same. Why? I have no idea, other than ignorance of their worth in God's eyes. Why would anyone choose the worst things in life as a good idea to live by? Jude warns us concerning these people. Jude 1:12 **These are the ones who are hidden reefs in your love feasts when they feast with you without fear, like shepherds caring only for themselves; clouds without water, carried along by winds; autumn trees without fruit, doubly dead, uprooted; 13 wild waves of the sea, churning up their own shameful deeds like dirty foam; wandering stars, for whom the gloom of darkness has been reserved forever.**

Thank God there is good news. We have been delivered from all of this death and darkness. Our Lord Jesus has taken away the sting of the mental torture that death can bring to a mind. 1Cor. 15:55

O death, where is your sting? O grave, where is your victory? The blood sacrifice Jesus offered of Himself on our behalf is the soul-saving balm we can apply to our hearts and consciousness. This allows us to let go of the fear death tries to bring into our minds. We have been set free from the chains death once had bound mankind with. The good news is that death, our last enemy, will be destroyed with all manner of evil on that great and glorious day of the Lord. Rev. 20:14a **Then death and the grave were thrown into the lake of fire.**

We are blessed that Jesus said we who are in Christ would be the light of the world. We are not a dark reflection of the human condition that Satan wants us to believe. Matt. 5:16 **In the same way, let your light shine before others, that they may see your good deeds and glorify your Father in heaven.** We have the choice to let the light of God's word lead us into the freedom Jesus came to give us through the finished work of the cross. Our Lord has given us His word, His armour, and His Holy Spirit to make sure we live a victorious life and are able to defeat the works of darkness. The truth does set us free from the dire judgment the world is under.

The Lord has given us eternal life, and what we do with that life is paramount to our living in peace. With Christ in our hearts, we can do more than just exist. We can live a fulfiled life led by the Holy Spirit. We can count on the fact that God wants us to be a living testimony of God's goodness, so that those who live in darkness may see there is a better choice in this life. Psalm 23:5a **You prepare a feast for me in the presence of my enemies.** What is worse than being dead is not living fully with the life God has given us. Be blessed and live free.

WHAT IS YOUR CHEAT?

Proverbs 11:1 The LORD detests the use of dishonest scales, but he delights in accurate weights.

The above Proverb says it plainly, "The Lord hates cheating and delights in honesty." A noncommittal attitude with no honest effort given to overcoming bad habits and strongholds in your life will not work. As a matter of fact, in most cases, the problem will get deeply entrenched and become harder to overcome because of the lazy spirit within the one who is in bondage. A sluggard learns to live with the personal prison that was made by his own attitude. Prov. 21:25 **The desire of the sluggard kills him, for his hands refuse to labor.**

"What is your cheat day? How many times a week do you get to cheat on your health system?" I have been asked these questions so many times over the last five years because of the large amount of weight I have lost and kept it off. My answer is, "I lost all the weight by the grace of God, and the strength He gave me to stay with the program the Lord laid out for me, and it did not include cheat days."

To regain my health, I had to stop cheating when it came to a lack of exercise and eating certain foods. There were no more gluttonous cheat days. It was my previous lifestyle of cheating that caused the illness in the first place. It was a lifestyle change God led me through and not another fad diet that brought health and self-control to my life.

If your first question is, "What is your cheat day?" then whatever it is you are wanting to overcome will not get done. Your focus is on cheating and not conquering. God detests cheating and that includes when you cheat yourself. Why would God participate in helping you cheat yourself out of the blessings of God? John 10:10b **I am come that they might have life, and that they might have it more abundantly.**

There is ridiculousness to wanting to start off a new life with an emphasis on a cheat day. It is like saying, "Okay Lord, now that you saved my soul, when can I get back to sinning? Once or twice a week would be nice. What do you think Lord? Does that work for you?" You would not say that to God and yet you do say it to yourself when it comes to overcoming hard things in your life. You are either in it to win it, or not at all. We are no longer children befuddled by all the sparkles and glitter. 1Cor. 13:11 **When I was a child, I spake as a child, I understood as a child, I thought as a child: but when I became a man, I put away childish things.**

This has become my cheat. I cheat the enemy of my soul by praying for the lost souls God puts on my heart. I cheat the devil by believing and praying by faith for the healing of those who are sick and suffering disease. I cheat the spirits of darkness by submitting to God and repenting when I sin. James 4:7 **Submit yourselves therefore to God. Resist the devil, and he will flee from you.** If you want a cheat day, then cheat the enemy out of having control in your life. Satan has been cheating the saints of God for centuries out of the blessings that are truly theirs.

Don't cheat yourself out of the blessings of God. Get rid of the dishonest scales you have been using to justify a cheating and shallow lifestyle. Start using the honest and accurate scales God has given you through grace to live within the blessings of God. After all, they are our blessings. Prov. 11:1 **The LORD detests the use of dishonest scales, but he delights in accurate weights.** God delights in your prosperity and overcoming attitude that is lived through Christ. By grace, say it, and mean it! "No more cheat days!" Amen.

SORE LOSERS

Proverbs 23:29 Who has woe? Who has sorrow? Who has strife? Who has complaints? Who has needless bruises? Who has bloodshot eyes?

I cannot think of a worse sore loser than Satan. He continually tries to give his slithering character to the human race, so that mankind becomes as miserable as he is. However, we have to make a righteous effort not to pick up his traits and methods. Sore losers always accuse others of their problems. Anything that goes wrong in their lives is a result of someone else's actions. Their accusation of "The reason the country has gone to shreds is that - this or that political party is in power." This rehashed complaint is their constant excuse for blaming all that is gone wrong for their own choices they made in life. The reason they can't get ahead is because of them. Satan has been providing fodder for sore losers throughout history.

In the garden of Eden, Satan surreptitiously accused God of holding back knowledge from Eve. Gen. 3:5 **For God knows that when you** eat of it your eyes will be opened, and you will be like God, knowing good and evil. Adam and Eve had all the knowledge they needed at the time to live a wholesome life. Satan tricked Eve into mistrusting the integrity of God, and she was deceived. The devil did this because he was and still is a jealous sore loser who wants to be greater than God. Isa. 14:13a You said in your heart, "I will ascend to the heavens; I will raise my throne above the stars of God. Thank the Lord for throwing Satan out of heaven forever. Luke 10:18 He said to them, "I watched Satan fall from heaven like lightning."

One of the oddest conversations regarding Satan's accusatory nature is found in the book of Job. We read the account of the devil accusing God and Job at the same time. The accusation claims that God is being unfair in how He protects Job from Satan's attacks. Like all sore losers, Satan cannot succeed in being destructive because it is God's fault. Job 1:10 Have you not put a hedge around him and his house and all that he has, on every side? You have blessed the work of his hands, and his possessions have increased in the land. The devil truly has a pathetic existence. To choose a rebellion against God and lose, plus try and break everything God makes, then have a tantrum in front of God accusing Him of His goodness, is absolute insanity.

Maybe sore losers are, to a degree, insane. Was it sane for Cain to become a sore loser and lose all he had through an act of revenge because God looked favourably on Abel's offering? Gen. 4:5 **But for Cain and his offering He had no regard. So Cain became very angry and his face was gloomy.** How had Cain's poor choices in life become Abel's fault? Like all sore losers, Cain had to find someone other than himself to accuse of the lack of character within his own soul.

In a slick way, the ten spies accused God of making them feel so small compared to the giants in the land of Canaan. They could not muster up the courage to go into the land God promised them. It was God's and the giant's fault the people of Israel could not fulfil their dreams. Num. 14:3a **Why is the LORD taking us to this country only to have us die in battle?** Even though God is for us, blaming all of our woes on Him is a way to deflect personal responsibility. The loser looks for excuses and says, "Why is God doing this to me? How can I ever get ahead if God is against me?" It sure sounds like something Satan would say.

So, let us answer the Proverb's questions. Prov.

23:29 **Who has woe? Who has sorrow? Who has strife? Who has complaints? Who has needless bruises? Who has bloodshot eyes?** Who has all these problems? Those who do not take personal responsibility for their lives, and those who do not take the proper actions within life. God has said in His word, that He is for us and has asked us to choose life and not the things that lead to death. The devil, on the other hand, will help anyone choose every possible failure available to them so that they become a loser like Satan is. The devil is trying to reproduce after his own kind. Do we really want to help the enemy's agenda? The choice is ours. How do you want to live? Josh. 24:15b **But as for me and my house, we will serve the LORD.** Amen!

MOCKERS AND SCOFFERS

Proverbs 9:7 The one who corrects a mocker will bring abuse on himself; the one who rebukes the wicked will get hurt.

The above verse speaks to the spirit of the day that the world is operating in. A spirit of mockery and scoffing at everything whether right or wrong. Sad to say, in many cases, the church is being influenced by the same spirit. Some of our church assemblies are becoming gathering places for scoffers and mockers who are abusing their fellow man because of what some congregants sincerely believe in their hearts. We know that the world's wickedness is far-reaching and hurts everything it touches. But the world's wickedness should not be practiced among the brothers and sisters in the Lord.

My concern is for the Christians who prattle on about complicated subjects they know nothing about. Without thought, they speak as though they are authorities on the subjects of science, politics, finances, and education. You would think every person expressing an opinion has a degree or doctorate in these sciences. They pontificate their canned rhetoric, as though they know all the answers to all problems in every field, when in fact they only have vague and unsound rehashed theories that have been posted and reposted on social media platforms. Prov. 18:2 **A fool takes no pleasure in understanding, but only in expressing his opinion.**

Rather than praying for our leaders in positions of authority that affect society as God instructs us to do, many within Christian circles condemn, tear apart, and promote lies in the same manner as the world does. This is not the spirit God gave us to minister in righteousness. We are to promote Godliness in life and not tear it down with a flood of nonsensical and useless words. 1Tim. 2:1 **I urge you, first of all, to pray for all people. Ask God to help them; intercede on their behalf, and give thanks for them. 2 Pray this way for kings and all who are in authority so that we can live peaceful and quiet lives marked by godliness and dignity.**

Real divisiveness takes place when someone tries to correct or instruct another person that may be promoting wrong information and adding to this world's problems rather than eliminating the woes within it. The reaction of the ones being corrected will result in either wisdom prevailing and hearts changing, or as the proverb says, the mocker abuses and hurts the one trying to sincerely help. Prov. 9:7 **The one who corrects a mocker will bring abuse on himself; the one who rebukes the wicked will get hurt.** The sad thing is, to choose to remain a recidivistic troglodyte by repeatedly mocking what is not understood when actual knowledge and help is available - is pathetic and an indictment against the intelligence God gave us.

As hard as this is for Christians to understand, we do not know and understand everything there is to know and understand. We are fortunate to know the God who does know all and understand all, therefore, this is why we pray to Him. I realize there is a lot of evil in the world and it can be frustrating to see it and feel like there is nothing we can do about it. But this is a lie of the enemy of our soul. When we read the burden of Habakkuk we see that he is going through the same thing we are experiencing today. Hab. 1:2 **How long, LORD, must I call for help, but you do not listen? Or cry out to you, "Violence!" but you do not save? 3 Why do you make me look at injustice? Why do you tolerate wrongdoing? Destruction and violence are before me; there is strife, and conflict abounds.**

Habakkuk does not just badmouth God and become condescending toward everyone around him or mock everything he did not understand. Instead, Habakkuk entered into what he did understand, and that is the declaration that God is God and He has the means and wisdom to deal with all mankind. Habakkuk decides to wait it out and see what God says about the situation rather than proclaim his ignorance to everyone on every social media platform. Hab. 2:1 **I will stand at my watch and station myself on the ramparts; I will look to see what He will say to me, and what answer I am to give to this complaint.**

Instead of mocking our leaders, try praying for them, because if you don't, you will only become angrier at all the things being done that are out of your control. Leave the scoffing and mocking to the people in the world and grow up in the spirit of our Lord. Why does Satan put so much time into laying traps to prevent people from praying for one another? Even that loser the devil knows how powerful praying Christians are when they become united under God. Christians do not have to agree with each other on everything in life, but living and praying in unity will destroy the works of the devil, and in a short time, misunderstandings will get settled and healings will take place. Psalm 133:1 **How good and pleasant it is when God's people live together in unity!**

Anyone can curse the darkness and complain bitterly about the world's problems. It takes very little intelligence to badmouth everything going on that is not understood. Mockers and scoffers will always be screaming their fears out loud. Since we are in Christ, the good news is that we have not been given the spirit of fear but rather the spirit of power and love. 2Tim. 1:7 **For God has not given us a spirit of fear, but of power and of love and of a sound mind.** Come on saints, let's use what God gave us to bring solutions to the world and peace in our hearts. Blessings.

CONDITIONED FOR CRUELTY

Proverbs 30:11 There is a generation that curses its father and does not bless its mother.

Galatians 6:7 **Do not be deceived: God is not mocked, for whatever one sows, that will he also reap.**

I'm paraphrasing here because this narrative is so off the wall. I think this is the gist of it. A news reporter was interviewing a recidivist criminal who was bemoaning the fact that it was not fair that his residence had been broken into and robbed while he was in custody for a crime he had committed. He felt the State should pay for his losses because they were holding him prisoner, while he was not at home to defend the stuff he had stolen from others. I must have heard the report wrong because surely, this is not where we have ended up in our reasoning. How has this become the commonsense of the day?

The attitude of entitlement that is now becoming a given in our society, which no longer holds people accountable for their actions, is the result of our nation reaping what has been sown throughout the last generation. Hos. 8:7a **For they have sown the wind, and they shall reap the whirlwind.** We have allowed the moral choices of the last few generations (mine included) to falter and be led by whatever felt good at the time, whether it was righteous or not. As my friend Scott says, "The formally accepted givens or basic standards that people lived by, have changed, and the commonsense givens that most people understood, are gone. The once caring expectations of uprightness that came through regular upbringing will have to be retaught to a generation who have been raised on violent imagery promoting cruel intent, and they have acquired their ethical values from everywhere and anything that seemed plausible at the time." To me, the scary part is that the generation who got their guidance from Beavis and Butt-Head and similar role models are now in charge of the levers that make the world work.

Every generation needs a God-inspired awakening so they can come through the difficulties of their day, and this generation is no different. We all need the reassurance of God's love and purpose for our lives. God's love can elevate a soul to choose life and find real righteous direction. The Lord's affection and salvation can pull a person out of despair and a visionless life. As the world system tries to equalize and make carbon copies of everyone through the philosophy of human-centredness, the authenticity of a person becomes muddied and uncertain. Plus, humanism, socialism, and authoritarianism in themselves cannot feed the hunger in a soul that was created to be fulfilled by God's eternal purposes. Instead, acts of cruelty become the results of all the emptiness people are experiencing as everyone lives by their own moral code.

As so many of you are wondering, I am also trying to understand, what are the governing authorities and bureaucratic departments counting on? What is their end game in trying to make everyone the same? What are they expecting as a result of converting everyone's thinking into a vegetative mundane state of existence? What are they counting on? I know a teacher who grinds her teeth when the subject of participation trophies for all comes up. She says, "What do we (as a society) expect when we are encouraging a generation of children who will not accelerate in trying to conquer the hard things that confront them? We give participation trophies for just signing up on a team, even though they do not show up to participate in half of the games. Then, these same kids (and their parents) feel entitled and expect the teachers to give away straight 'A' grades on their report cards even though they have not done the work. Where has this dullness of thought come from?" I think this dullness of thought has come from a few generations sowing sinfulness and expecting liberation.

Prov. 30:11a **There is a generation that curses its....** leaders, teachers, neighbours, nurses, and anyone who has a genuine thought of kindness. The ever-increasing cruelty in life that we are watching unfold has become the world's inheritance. These acts of selfishness are people's expressions of what is in their hearts. Out of the heart will flow the issues of life. Luke 6:45b **For the mouth speaks what the heart is full of.** We are watching the crumbling of human resolve and strength fall apart. What we are seeing and hearing would have been thought insane at one time but is now mainstream thinking for many. The self-righteous declaration of "If it feels right, then do it," regardless of how destructively it affects others, has come back to bite humanity with consequential results. Meditating on cruelty and acting out what the cruelty expressed has become the given within a confused society. Prov. 1:16 **They rush to commit evil deeds. They hurry to commit murder.**

Stop Watering Dead Plants

We are not the only ones who have ever gone through this mess and felt the heaviness of the times. Habukkuk was written around 586-BC. Habukkuk is describing the very same things we are witnessing daily. Hab. 1:2 **How long, O LORD, will I call for help, and You will not hear? I cry out to You, "Violence!" Yet You do not save. 3 Why do You make me see disaster, and make me look at destitution? Yes, devastation and violence are before me; strife exists and contention arises. 4 Therefore the Law is ignored, and justice is never upheld. For the wicked surround the righteous; therefore justice comes out confused.** Confused is right! How true a statement that the world is confused and without remedy.

The Lord said that we would have trials and sorrows, but to be courageous because He has overcome the world and all the cruelty in it. We are to take heart in that fact. Jesus is letting us know that He has overcome so that we may have peace on this earth. John 16:33 **I have told you all this so that you may have peace in me. Here on earth you will have many trials and sorrows. But take heart, because I have overcome the world.** One translation says, "Be of good cheer I have overcome the world." Be courageous, be of good cheer, and take heart when we see all the cruel and unjust events taking place around us because the Lord has overcome the one who is causing the mayhem. Be assured, that Satan's days are numbered.

God asks us to meditate on what Jesus said because His faith-filled words will bring peace to our hearts and minds in the center of all the chaos. If we keep our eyes on the Lord, then the woes of the world will be a noise in the background as we walk with our God. We overcome because Christ has already overcome the hellish disorder that brings distress to our hearts. Keep praying for the loss and one another, and trust in the Lord's victory, then the peace of God will be our peace Amen!

STUMBLING BLOCKS

Proverbs 26:27 Whoever digs a pit will fall into it, and a stone will come back on him who starts it rolling.

Hebrews 12:1b **Let us throw off everything that hinders and the sin that so easily entangles. And let us run with perseverance the race marked out for us.** The statement of caution we are to take notice of - is, "Let us throw off the sin that so easily entangles us." We all have that sin or those transgressions that so easily cause us to stumble. I know someone who fights jealousy to the point of crying about it. I know of a person who cannot stop visiting gambling facilities and is repenting regularly for wasting so much money that he knows God has blessed him with. A few sipping-saints have reported that they are having difficulty stopping their use of alcohol. All these activities are not a problem until they are! Yes, I have my nemesis too. We all seem to have something that just beats us up and reminds us of our constant need for our saviour.

Someone might say, "The temptations

mentioned above are not a problem to me at all."
I could agree with that, but at the same time, we
need to realize that what becomes a demonic
dragged-out war for one person is not a big
deal for another to withstand the temptation.
Meanwhile, the sins you fall for might seem so
lame to others as they roll their eyes wondering
why you just can't get it together. There is always
something we are trying to overcome and we
cannot do it alone. We need Jesus at all times in
all sinful situations to help keep us in the light of
His grace. Eph. 2:8 **For you are saved by grace
through faith, and this is not from yourselves;
it is God's gift** — 9 **not from works, so that no
one can boast.**

Even when winning our battle over sin, it is
God's grace at work within us. Defeating sin is
not accomplished through our willpower alone.
Sin, iniquity, and transgressions are overcome
through the blood and sacrifice of the Lord
working within our free will so we can walk in
Christ's righteousness. It is all God's redemptive
grace and finished work at the cross that gives us
the power to overcome any stronghold. The Lord
even dresses us up in His righteous armour so we
can fight the battles the enemy throws at us. Eph.
6:10 **Finally, be strong in the Lord and in His
mighty power.** 11 **Put on the full armor of**

God, so that you can take your stand against the devil's schemes.

Cain's stumbling block of jealousy toward his brother Abel, got the better of him because he would not listen to what God was saying. The Lord's warning that sin was crouching at the door of Cain's heart and the sin of jealous anger was waiting to destroy him. Cain rejected God's loving admonition, and the result was that jealousy won the battle. Gen. 4:10 **But the LORD said, "What have you done? Listen! Your brother's blood cries out to me from the ground!** God's warnings are for us to hear and work out with His guidance so we can defeat the sin that so easily entangles us. It is not a one-time fight and that trespass is destroyed forever. No, it is spiritual warfare that we engage in every time the temptation shows up to tempt our souls again. The good news is through Christ we can win the battles. Phil. 4:13 **I can do all things through Christ which strengtheneth me.**

King Saul's insecurity and inferiority caused him to become jealous of David because of a few song lyrics exalting the battle David won over the Philistines. 1Sam. 18:8 **Then Saul became very angry, for this lyric displeased him; and he said, "They have given David credit for ten thousands, but to me they have given credit**

for only thousands! Now what more can he have but the kingdom?" Saul was inventing a kingdom takeover by David that did not exist. It was all in Saul's mind causing his imagination to create problems where there were none. His insecurities were an entrance for the devil to create jealousies and anger to manifest. The sin of jealousy then created the sin of hatred and murderous rage in Saul's heart. Sin begets sin, and if we do not deal with the sin that so easily entangles us, it leads to uglier transgressions.

Another stumbling block the enemy of our soul uses - is when we sin, Satan tries to cause us to hate ourselves. This is such a successful tactic. If Satan can get us into self-loathing, it can be a long way back to redemption because we cannot shake the ugly image we have created of ourselves. Meanwhile, God is in love with us, wanting us to come to Him with a repentant heart so we can defeat the works of the devil. While tangled in sin, we tend to forget that Jesus defeated Satan, death, and hell with His perfect sacrifice of Himself on the cross. Rev. 1:18 **I am the Living One; I was dead, and now look, I am alive for ever and ever! And I hold the keys of death and Hades.** This battle has already been won by God. We need to use our faith and act within the Lord's master plan that overcomes any iniquity that becomes a battleground for our souls.

If anyone has fallen into sin, then get up, and repent. God has won our eternal souls, and our names are written in the Lord's scarred hands and the book of eternal life. Don't let the failures we have experienced sour the multiple blessings that we live in and that await us through Christ our Lord. We are more than conquerors in Him. Yes, there are stumbling blocks in life, but there are far more victories that await us in Jesus name. Amen!

Norm Sawyer

PART 1:

QUESTIONS FOR UNDERSTANDING

1. *What did you learn in this section of the book?*
2. *What surprised you the most?*
3. *What subject(s) spoke to your heart?*
4. *Did the material that you read help you understand the subject(s) more or less?*
5. *What topics are important to you? Why?*
6. *How do these articles relate to you?*
7. *After reading this section of the book, what will you change in your life?*

PART TWO:

PERSPECTIVE

Stop Watering Dead Plants

We all have a way of seeing things and we have to understand that others have a perspective on life's issues as well. We need to let God teach us to hear each other. Rom. 12:18 If it is possible, as far as it depends on you, live at peace with everyone.

PERSPECTIVE

Proverbs 18:17 The one who states his case first seems right, until the other comes and examines him.

Within two days, I heard odd statements describing beauty in opposite terms. A friend was visiting from Louisiana and had noticed some very tall tulips in full bloom. She said, "Those flowers are so beautiful they look fake." She had to touch them to make sure they were real flowers. The next day, I was at a business establishment servicing a piece of equipment when I heard a customer say to the proprietor, "Those fake flowers look so real I can't tell the difference." She had to touch them to be assured they were artificial flowers. It struck me that things are not as they seem. We tend to take things at face value, and once we believe something is real or not, It can be difficult to change our perspective on that belief.

The strange thing about perspective is how some people can end up with a point of view that just seems ludicrous. The world is flat theory, has a worldwide following, and they have explanations galore to explain away the ability of ships on the sea and planes in the air that circumnavigate around the world. Big pharma and governments are making sure that all Chemtrails in our skies are filled with toxic chemicals to control the shopping habits of society. Alien Lizard people live among us and are plotting a takeover by introducing climate change to suit their climatized needs to live here and take over the planet. I'm sure you have heard some of your friends and family come up with some of the most unbelievable ideas and perspectives out there. 2Tim. 4:3 **For a time is coming when people will no longer listen to sound and wholesome teaching. They will follow their own desires and will look for teachers who will tell them whatever their itching ears want to hear.**

Our understanding and beliefs can be adjusted by the Holy Spirit if we let God sow His truth within us. Saul of Tarsus was on his way to condemn the new Christians for stating, "Jesus Christ is the Lord." His perspective changed when God knocked Saul off his horse and revealed Himself to Saul as Christ the Lord of the church and the universe. Acts 9:4 **He fell to the ground and heard a voice saying to him, "Saul! Saul! Why are you persecuting me?"** 5 **"Who are** you, lord?" Saul asked. And the voice replied, **"I am Jesus, the one you are persecuting!"** Not only did the Lord help Saul change his perspective of who Jesus is, but the understanding of Jesus as our saviour was so profound that it changed Saul's perspective of his own life and he became known as Paul the Apostle.

As ambient light hinders us from seeing the stars at night, so do the ambient attractions of worldliness hinder us and may change our perspective from seeing the glorious light of the Lord that He asks us to walk in. If you believe God is out to get you, then no matter how much you try to satisfy God, your outlook on life will be arduous and bleak. If you believe that Jesus is Lord and you have been set free through Christ's sacrifice, then your standpoint of faith will give you peace and freedom throughout your life. Only after the Lord has revealed His goodness to us can we take on a new view of who Jesus is and discard what the enemy of our soul has been lying to us about all our lives. Prov. 18:17 **The one who states his case first seems right, until the other comes and examines him.** God's perspective of us is a wonder to behold.

I have been asked many times why I read the bible regularly and why I promote the idea of staying current by reading God's word. My explanation is simple. Through the illumination of the Holy Spirit, who reveals His word to me, I get to see how God sees me and the perspective I need to have about myself. We can get a glimpse through God's eyes of what He sees in us. Even though it is through a glass darkly or a mirrored reflection as the word explains it, we can get a perspective of God's love that He has for us. 1Cor. 13:12 **For now we see only a reflection as in a mirror, but then face to face. Now I know in part, but then I will know fully, as I am fully known.** How good is that? To have a sense of peace that we are loved and can call on God's name at any time, and to know that He hears us because our perspective of Him is based on His love for us and not what we do. I like that. Blessings upon us all.

A-I AND I

Proverbs 21:30 There is no wisdom, no insight, no plan that can succeed against the LORD.

In his book, *The Price Of Tomorrow*, Jeff Booth makes an observation, explaining the impact of AI artificial intelligence on the economy, jobs, and the life changes that will occur because of the staggering effect on our ability to keep up with the fast acceleration of change. When AI is compared to the advent of electricity becoming available for the world's use and the effect it had on human history, AI will be - If electricity was a match, artificial intelligence is the sun. Dan. 12:4 **But you, Daniel, keep these words secret and seal the book until the time of the end. Many will roam about, and knowledge will increase.** Like most world-changing innovations we eventually catch up and adjust our lives to the technologies available. However, the hypothesis in the case of AI is that we may not catch up, or it may take us a long time to do so.

I was listening to a news report explaining how fifty-two mortgage brokers who worked for a major bank in Toronto had been replaced by two people who manage an algorithm that could do the same output of work and diagnosis as to whether the applicants for mortgages qualified. One of the major observations is that AI will be affecting the middle-class lifestyle more than other workers because of all the clerical work that will be replaced. In the same report, they went on to explain that from all the legal files now available online, law firms are starting to use software to find cases and precedents needed to declare in court. There is no need for the same amount of paralegals who once did this work. Plus, this work is being accomplished at record speeds that the paralegal cannot compete with, and the time saved in work hours gives law firms greater profit-margin.

Of course, the mortgage brokers and paralegals who owe on their student loans, are now scrambling for and competing with those who normally apply for entry-level service jobs, thus causing disruptions for the first-time job finders. These indebted professionals have to pay off their student loans while they consider new loans (a vicious circle) to take new courses in other career choices that may also fall redundant to the advancements of artificial intelligence. A lot of those who have been affected end up moving back in with their parents because the cost of living is overwhelming. Rev. 6:6a **Then I heard what sounded like a voice among the four living creatures, saying, "Two pounds of wheat for a day's wages, and six pounds of barley for a day's wages.** All because of the fast and changing technological advancement coming in at lightning speeds.

It is difficult for many of the youth to make career choices for what is not known will be needed in the future. Some young people are graduating after years of study, only to find out their chosen field and the work that was available when they started the courses have been replaced with algorithms. No one saw it coming, including the faculties of the institutions of learning. In some cases, the need for a workforce for that area of service that was chosen no longer exists. These are the dilemmas our next generations are faced with. The wisdom that these future students will need will have to be divinely inspired wisdom to know what to do for a lifetime career. Prov. 9:10 **Fear of the LORD is the foundation of wisdom. Knowledge of the Holy One results in good judgment.**

After fifty and some years that I have been in business, I have had to contend with change.

Stop Watering Dead Plants

When I started in the sales department of my company, the average business had an adding machine, a typewriter, and a black rotary phone on a desk. The high-tech office might have a Gestetner machine for rolling off multiple copies of documents. Then the first thermal roll paper photocopy machines came along, and the electric typewriters started showing up, plus a flashy digital display calculator. Green or orange word display screens on small monitors connected to big computers started replacing the typewriters and plain paper copiers were the had-to-have in every office. The thermal fax machine replaced the noisy teleprinters, and on it went until many of my contemporary salesmen were replaced with robotic phone services.

Yes, change is inevitable, and it comes along whether we like it or not. I was the one selling a lot of these new office products and kept up with all the advancements until recently when company policy changed and started phasing out the need for sales reps. After all, anything can be ordered within seconds on any connected device. I am fortunate because the older owners of the said companies I serviced for years wanted to keep using their old equipment until they shut down, and servicing those office products is something I know how to do. So, as strange as it turned out,

I have a small niche business fixing and servicing all kinds of older office equipment. Therefore, AI and I get along.

Artificial intelligence will never replace our soul's desire to serve the Lord. All the God-haters, who will misuse AI because of their arrogant visions of grandeur, will be like those who participated in building the Tower of Babel. With sorcery and the advancements of their day, they tried to play God, but they ended up dispersed, confused and lost in their communication. Gen. 11:7 **Come, let us go down and confuse their language so they will not understand each other.** Thus babbling their way to the next time they tried to be better than God.

There is no man-made technological plan or insight that can outwit the Lord or come close to God's eternal genius. Prov. 21:30 **There is no wisdom, no insight, no plan that can succeed against the LORD.** What we see as advanced artificial intelligence and the threatening changes that may occur because of it, will still be child's play to our Mighty God. Look to the Lord for wisdom as to what to do with the inevitable changes of life coming our way. Life with God goes on and it is good. Amen!

WE CAN SPIN IT!

Proverbs 28:6 Better the poor person who lives with integrity than the rich one who distorts right and wrong.

He who distorts right and wrong plus spins the truth into half-truths lacks integrity. Spin-masters distort, rewrite, and exaggerate the reported news to suit the people presenting a slanted version of events that took place. Psalm 12:2 **They speak vanity every one with his neighbour: with flattering lips and with a double heart do they speak.** Professional spin-masters work tirelessly to make the news events speak favorably to the sensibilities of the targeted group. Distorted news or fake news as many call it, is believed to be a modern day media problem. There has always been fake news throughout history. There is nothing new here.

The Jewish leaders declared, "We can spin it." Matt. 28:12 **After the priests had assembled with the elders and agreed on a plan, they gave the soldiers a large sum of money 13 and told them, "Say this, 'His disciples came**

during the night and stole him while we were sleeping.' The chief priests were creating fake news about what had really happened to the body of Jesus. This is one of the biggest spins ever told. From that fateful day, the distorted report of the Resurrection of Jesus has been lied about, wrongly reported on, and incorrectly taught. The master of spin, the devil, has been weaving stories for gullible people who live in deception.

Part of the problem is that people want to hear what they want to hear. "Don't give me the truth. I can't handle it." This is their reply to anything that interferes with their life choices. Tell me what I want to hear so I can keep on sinning to my heart's content. 2Tim. 4:3 **For the time will come when they will not endure sound doctrine; but after their own lusts shall they heap to themselves teachers, having itching ears; 4 and they shall turn away their ears from the truth, and shall be turned unto fables.** When you have a willing participant to the deception of life, then there will be no problem for Satan to step in and fill your head with whatever it is you want to hear.

Gainsayers and bold face liars have been spinning different versions of God's salvation plan from day one. The distortion of truth, right and wrong, is the agenda of those who would turn the grace of the Lord into a free for all. Jude 1:4 **For there are certain men crept in unawares, who were before of old ordained to this condemnation, ungodly men, turning the grace of our God into lasciviousness, and denying the only Lord God, and our Lord Jesus Christ.**

Grace teaches us to observe the word of God and to keep it in our hearts. Titus 2:11 **For the grace of God that brings salvation hath appeared to all men, 12 teaching us that, denying ungodliness and worldly lusts, we should live soberly, righteously, and godly, in this present world.** Grace does not give us permission to sin. On the contrary, it teaches us to avoid it. When the Lord is the Lord of our heart, no spin is needed to explain our choices of righteousness in God.

We don't have to worry about keeping the story straight or keeping the spin according to group agendas. Truth is the truth, right is right, and wrong is wrong. No spin is needed. We can let our yes be yes, and our no be no. Matt. 5:37 **But let your 'yes' mean 'yes,' and your 'no' mean 'no.' Anything more than this is from the evil one.** We don't have to spin the word of the Lord. We just have to proclaim it and the word of God will do what God intends it to do. Isa. 55:11 **So**

my word that comes from my mouth will not return to me empty, but it will accomplish what I please and will prosper in what I send it to do.

Thank God the Lord was truthful with us when he sent Jesus to save us from eternal death. He did not have to spin anything. He demonstrated His love for us through the sacrifice of Jesus. A plain and straight declaration of His love. Thank you, God, for Jesus.

TRIBALISM

Proverbs 29:11 A fool gives full vent to his anger, but a wise person holds it in check.

Tribalism according to the dictionary: The behavior and attitudes that stem from strong loyalty to one's own tribe, party, or social group.

The religion of tribalism is flourishing. The world's population is merging into different camps of belief that are available to those who want to take part in something they can relate to. There does not have to be any logic, common sense, or even an altruistic purpose within the movements of these tribal structures. The fact is, that these tribal entities exist and are available to be joined by anyone.

At this time in North America, we have the tribes of the far left and distant right political parties fulminating on every sentence being spoken. We also have the vaccinated versus the not vaccinated pointing out each other's false claims. Plus, the no masks demonstrators versus those wearing masks have squared off in bitter arguments, separating friends and families. Our ability to control our emotions is becoming no better than the thugs who break everything and fight after the loss of an international soccer game. We are bringing this spirit into our homes, neighbourhoods, and churches. All because we want to give someone an angry piece of our mind. Prov. 29:11a **A fool gives full vent to his anger.**

Some tribal members are picking battles that are lost before they start, and yet, they put their whole souls into the fight. A few boisterous souls are fighting for their belief that the world is flat. To me, this seems to be a battle that will just go round in circles. Thank God that members of *The Flat Earth Tribe* do not work for NASA, at least I don't think they do. What is causing people to drop their guard and become advocates for nonsense and are expressing personal rage to fight for absolute foolishness? 2Tim. 4:3 **For the time will come when people will not tolerate sound doctrine, but according to their own desires, will multiply teachers for themselves because they have an itch to hear what they want to hear.**

There is nothing new here. The Apostle Paul had the same problems to deal with. The political parties of his day maintained a religious portfolio that was daily present to the people. The Herodians were members of Herod's government watchdogs making sure taxes were paid, and insurrections did not take place. Judaism was represented by the Scribes and Pharisees who hung out with the Herodians to find out what the ruling class was up to. Circumcision had become a sharp divisive argument among those who were doing church in a new way. Lost in all of it, was the love for God, and the eternal love that God has for mankind.

Paul had to address the dangers of tribalism slipping into the church. There were those who felt their tribe was more significant because they had been led to the Lord by Paul, where others had only been led to the Lord by some of the other leaders. Thus creating a tribal instinct that had to be quashed within the hearts of the new Christians. 1Cor. 3:4 **For whenever someone says, "I belong to Paul," and another, "I belong to Apollos," are you not acting like mere humans? 5 What then is Apollos? What is Paul? They are servants through whom you believed, and each has the role the Lord has given.**

The enemy of our soul has been dividing people from the first day that man was created. We who are in Christ have to realize that people will have different persuasions that they will feel comfortable with throughout their life. However, we are not to make these sidebar ideologies our gods. The Apostle Paul had a solution for the differences he was coming up against. He remained in Christ while reaching out to the people and bringing Jesus into the belief that some were so passionately expressing. 1Cor. 9:20a **When I was with the Jews, I lived like a Jew to bring the Jews to Christ. 22 To the weak I became weak, that I might win the weak. I have become all things to all people, that by all means I might save some.**

Paul did not get overwhelmed by all the different trains of thought, but rather, he brought Christ into the person's belief, thereby allowing Jesus to deal with all the fears, uncertainties, political views, and even the nonsense of the day that the person was living in. When Jesus is the Lord of our life, stuff will get straightened out in our life. Jesus was and still is the answer for dealing with the wars and conflicts within people's hearts. If we would allow the Lord to straighten out our doctrines and beliefs, we would not get suckered into arguing about all the narratives going on around us that Satan continually promotes. Real peace would be our guide, and we would leave the bitterness caused by all the vitriol to the trolls who sow all manner of discourse.

It might be time to leave the tribe you have been foolheartedly speaking for. If we have to identify as a tribe, then let us become full citizens within God's kingdom where there is no doubt who the King of kings and Lord of lords is. The light of our Lord, can stab any darkness and rip apart the gloom that has enveloped a heart or mind. Jesus makes us one by His Spirit. We can extend the hand of fellowship with patience toward those who are grappling with their maturity in Christ. We all need to be extra patient with each other because God is not finished with us. We are all an ongoing project in God's salvation plan. Jude 1:24 **Now all glory to God, who is able to keep you from falling away and will bring you with great joy into His glorious presence without a single fault.** Let us receive our peace through Christ for the day we are living in. Amen and amen!

YOU CAN'T GO BACK

Proverbs 7:19 For the goodman is not at home, he is gone a long journey.

The longing we Christians often feel in our hearts for home is a longing for the time we will be living with our Lord in eternity. This feeling of homesickness is often manifested in spending all we have on the dream home, kitchen, and other merchandise. We sometimes invest all emotion and money into moving to the dream country that seems to have a welcoming culture where we think we will fit in.

We end up looking for an unattainable peace of mind because of the frantic and hectic lives we live. Literally, looking for peace in all the wrong places. We think of this dream life way over there somewhere. If we could just find it, we would finally be home.

We come up with these unrealistic comparisons of joy and peace from our youth and days gone by when things were so much better. The problem is that our hearts and memories are very selective and we end up creating a fantasy past of joviality and a life that was so much easier to live. Eccl. 7:10 **Do not say, "Why were the old days better than these?" For it is not wise to ask such questions.**

The word of God asks us not to say, "Things were better way back when," but to look forward to the blessing and preparation of the eternal home our Lord and Savior has prepared for us. John 14:2 **My Father's house has many rooms; if that were not so, would I have told you that I am going there to prepare a place for you? 3 And if I go and prepare a place for you, I will come back and take you to be with me that you also may be where I am.** Being where Jesus dwells is home.

Our human nature is to find a comfortable place and live there. However, the Spirit of God compels us to move forward with His plan for His kingdom here on earth and it often causes chafing to our comfort zones to the point of unease. We start looking in the rear-view mirror thinking we have left something important behind. Because our focus is in the rear-view mirror, we run amuck on the road ahead of us messing up the plan God has for us. We then sit there crying for the good old days and lose the vision God had in our hearts. Ex. 16:3a **The Israelites said to them, "If only we had died by the LORD's**

hand in Egypt! There we sat around pots of meat and ate all the food we wanted.

How interesting that the Israelites had already forgotten they had been slaves under extreme bondage and now they were longing at selective memories of a moment in time, from way back when. Num. 11:5 **We remember the fish we ate in Egypt at no cost--also the cucumbers, melons, leeks, onions and garlic.** Is that what you remember? Let me ask you this question, oh Israelites: "Do you remember this prayer to your God?" Ex. 2:23 **During those many days the king of Egypt died, and the people of Israel groaned because of their slavery and cried out for help.** Their cry for rescue from slavery came up to God.

The Israelites had forgotten they were where they were because they had asked God to help them out of bondage in Egypt. Are we not doing the same thing? We ask Jesus to come into our hearts and be our Lord and Savior. Then God does what we ask and life changes from that moment on.

Of course things are going to change, and some of the changes will be at odds with our thinking because we are not God. We are not going to continue living our old way of life. The Lord is going to help us become a son of the living God. Psalm 32:8 **I will instruct you and teach you in the way you should go; I will counsel you with my loving eye on you.**

It is interesting that a lot of counseling that pastors and counselors do for people are basically reminding the people that they are where they are because they prayed and God answered their prayers. Then with indignation, they say, "That is not how I wanted the prayer answered! I was better off back then." Oh really? Back then when you were on your way to hell and were strung-out on all kinds of addictive substances and behaviors? Back then when you were friendless and making life choices from a weak and corrupted conscience?

No, saints. You cannot go back to the good old days. You are here today and now. Psalm 118:24 **This is the day the Lord has made; We will rejoice and be glad in it.** The longing for home is a righteous feeling because it is engrafted into our spirit through the work of the cross. Phil. 3:20 **But our citizenship is in heaven. And we eagerly await a Savior from there, the Lord Jesus Christ, 21 who, by the power that enables him to bring everything under his control, will transform our lowly bodies so that they will be like his glorious body.**

As odd as it sounds, we are Pilgrims in a strange land because the earth groans under the weight of sin right now. Rom. 8:22 **We know that the whole creation has been groaning as in the pains of childbirth right up to the present time.**

When the Lord establishes the new heaven and new earth we will say with a full heart, "I am home. Praise you Lord Jesus, praise your wonderful name, for I am truly home." Keep the eyes of your heart looking forward to where God is leading because you are truly getting closer to home. May the peace of God fill your heart with the joy of the Lord. In Jesus name.

A REAL TRUST

Proverbs 29:25 The fear of man brings a snare: but whoso puts his trust in the Lord shall be safe.

The fear of man brings confusion when we try to have faith in God. We read all through the book of Exodus that God, without doubt, is leading the children of Israel to the promised land in order to possess it and move in, fully. God's intention was not to bring them to the border of the promised land and say, sorry we just can't go in. Something happened to stop the conquering agenda that God had for His chosen people.

Right at the appointed time for the promise to be fulfilled, the Israelites chose to believe the lies of ten of the twelve spies. Num. 13:32 **And they brought up an evil report of the land which they had searched unto the children of Israel, saying, The land, through which we have gone to search it, is a land that eats up the inhabitants thereof; and all the people that we saw in it are men of a great stature.** Yet, in Verse 30 **And Caleb stilled the people before Moses, and said, Let us go up at once, and**

possess it; for we are well able to overcome it.

The rebellion began to take root because of the fear of man. Num.13:33 **And there we saw the giants, the sons of Anak, which come of the giants: and we were in our own sight as grasshoppers, and so we were in their sight.** It seemed that it was easier for the Israelites to believe in the misery of ten fearful men, than to have hope in the God-given battle cry of the two brave soldiers of God. The fear of man will stop you from moving forward in the vision of the Lord, and life.

How often have we not entered the promise of God that was clearly given to our hearts? We came to a place of doubt, because it was taking longer than we thought it should. So we started replacing the vision with one of our own. We see this in the story of Saul who had been commanded by God, through Samuel, to utterly destroy every Amalekite, their animals, and every possession they owned. Totally rid them from off the earth.

The judgment of God toward the Amalekites was pronounced and it was to be carried out by the army of Israel. 1Sam. 15:3a **Now go and smite Amalek, and utterly destroy all that they have.** Saul did not do what God said, but did it his way. 1Sam:15:9a **But Saul and the people spared Agag, and the best of the sheep, and of the** oxen, and of the fatlings, and the lambs, and all that was good.

Partial obedience is not obedience, and this heart attitude caused Saul to lose his kingdom. 1Sam. 13:26 **And Samuel said unto Saul, I will not return with thee: for thou hast rejected the word of the LORD, and the LORD hath rejected thee from being king over Israel.** The fear of man stopped the destiny of Saul's kingdom. 1Sam. 15:24 **And Saul said unto Samuel, I have sinned: for I have transgressed the commandment of the LORD, and thy words: because I feared the people, and obeyed their voice.** What have we sacrificed in life because of the fear of man or the fear of what THEY might think?

The fear of man will cause shame to manifest in our hearts and we will lose our strength toward a God-given vision. Peter, who earlier in the week had declared his unwavering love for Christ, was ashamed and fearful days later. This resulted in Peter denying he even knew Christ. Mark 14:67 **And when she saw Peter warming himself, she looked upon him, and said, And thou also wast with Jesus of Nazareth.** Mark 14:71 **But he began to curse and to swear, saying, I know not this man of whom ye speak.**

The fear of man will keep us in a place of

uncertain apprehension and bitterness. Once this bitterness takes root, shame will grow in strength. Mark 14:72b **Thou shalt deny me thrice. And when he thought thereon, he wept.** Thank God there is forgiveness on this side of the cross. Rev. 1:5 **And from Jesus Christ, who is the faithful witness, and the first begotten of the dead, and the prince of the kings of the earth. Unto him that loved us, and washed us from our sins in his own blood.**

The fear of man comes when we have something to hide and we are unrepentant of our sin. Eph. 4:27 **Neither give place to the devil.** My son gave this response to his friends when they asked him why he got along so well with his parents. This happened at a party so he had all their attention when he said, "I get along with my parents because I have nothing to hide from them." I thought his statement was profound for a young man in high school.

Why can we put our total trust in this salvation of the Lord? Num. 23:19 **God is not a man, that he should lie; neither the son of man, that he should repent: hath he said, and shall he not do it? or hath he spoken, and shall he not make it good?** That is a real blessed assurance because this truth will cause us to believe the love God has for us. 1John 4:16 **And we have known**

and believed the love that God hath to us. God is love; and he that dwells in love dwells in God, and God in him.

Fear crushes the spirit of man, but trust in the Lord keeps our souls safely grounded in Him who first loved us. I trust my Lord Jesus.

CONFIDENCE OF HEART

Proverbs 3:26 For the LORD shall be thy confidence, and shall keep thy foot from being taken.

The clear rustling sound that came from the undergrowth and dead foliage that covered the jungle floor was unsettling to the primal fears that lurked in the deep subconscious of my mind. Phil, Leonardo and I were walking toward the rented Jeep, when a tarantula the size of a man's hand went scurrying to our right at a very rapid pace. Moving faster toward us the spider darted over and under fallen palm leaves, moving these obstacles at will.

Increasingly our insecurities grew, but as the prehistoric hunter rapidly changed direction our nervousness eased. "Hokie-Dina, did you see the size of that thing?" Phil said. The relief was evident in his voice. "It kind of makes the hair on the back of your neck stand up, doesn't it?" I said, with equal relief that the tarantula had moved on to stalk something more its size.

We then turned and saw that we were surrounded by the Mayan ruins of Tikal in

Guatemala Central America. The sense of awe that these ancient ruins emanated was a feeling that you had personally discovered these extremely old temples for the first time, even though they had been seen for hundreds of years and by thousands of people. I kept thinking of the confidence of belief it would have taken to build these stone giants. Not unlike the city of Babel.

Gen. 11:4 **And they said, Go to, let us build us a city and a tower, whose top may reach unto heaven; and let us make us a name, lest we be scattered abroad upon the face of the whole earth.** Confidence in God will accomplish what God has put in our hearts, but when slightly corrupted by personal gain we are soon building our own kingdoms where God cannot find room to live.

When God saw what the citizens were up to when they were building a city that focused on mystical powers, the Lord said that there was nothing that could stop their progress - even though it was contrary to the Lord's wishes. Gen. 11:6 **And the LORD said, Behold, the people is one, and they have all one language; and this they begin to do: and now nothing will be restrained from them, which they have imagined to do.**

After God's intervention the city was stopped and what remained was called Babel. When God directs the programme, the will of God gets done. Psalm 118:8 **It is better to trust in the LORD than to put confidence in man.**

How many God-given ideas turned into a babbling mess when we started adding our own know-how to the plan when it was clearly given in the first place? Before we came to our senses there were cost overruns and unforeseen legal problems. So we lose confidence in God, turn to more human know-how, and start a fund-raiser to save God's plan from the enemy. Meanwhile, God is patiently waiting for us to get back to His original plan that was cost-efficient and legal. Psalm 37:5 **Commit thy way unto the LORD; trust also in him; and he shall bring it to pass.**

What is it about mankind and Christians alike that we repeat the mantra of Babel? "Let us build us a city and a tower, whose top may reach unto heaven." We do this over and over even when God is sowing His vision in the hearts of His saints. Why do we think God is going to do it the exact same way as He did it the last time?

I'm not saying God can't do it the same way. I'm just wondering why we think He must do it that way. Confidence in God is confidence in

God's character, not in a formula for successful living. Confidence in God is just that: confidence that God loves and hears us. 1John 5:14 **And this is the confidence that we have in him, that, if we ask any thing according to his will, he hears us: 15 And if we know that he hear us, whatsoever we ask, we know that we have the petitions that we desired of him.**

If my confidence is not in God, then I run the risk that I will become overconfident in myself and become hubris of heart and mind, walking without God's peace. We need to build a life that is glorifying to God. With His help, we will. Matt. 6:19 **Lay not up for yourselves treasures upon earth, where moth and rust doth corrupt, and where thieves break through and steal: 20 But lay up for yourselves treasures in heaven, where neither moth nor rust doth corrupt, and where thieves do not break through nor steal: 21 For where your treasure is, there will your heart be also.** Amen.

THE PETER MOMENT

Proverbs 20:9 Who can say, "I have kept my heart pure; I am clean and without sin"?

Have you ever experienced that Peter moment when Jesus turns and looks you in the eye? When you mess up and sin, and in the moment of knowing that fact, an ominous Peter moment comes upon you. Luke 22:61 **And the Lord turned and looked at Peter. Then Peter remembered the word the Lord had spoken to him: "Before the rooster crows today, you will deny Me three times." 62 And he went outside and wept bitterly.** We have all been disappointed in ourselves for missing the mark God has set before us. The realization of it is as if Jesus looks at you in the eyes and you know that you know you need to repent.

That moment after denying God by disobeying Him is when the conviction of God's love persuades our hearts to repent. The repentance must be on God's terms, however, many times our flesh wants to rise with a promise to God that from that moment on, we will be the soul of exactitude and will never fall again, but, like the empty promises of an alcoholic who is in denial, we do fall again. Our flesh always wants to take over the repentance process. The Holy Spirit directs us to repent, and we start directing the parameters and conditions of our repentance. Prov. 20:9 **Who can say, "I have kept my heart pure; I am clean and without sin"?** Will we ever get out of God's redemptive way and let Him do His work in us? God's forgiving grace is life-giving and will establish the assurance of faith within us. How can any man manufacture that amazing grace?

We do not want to be the reason or give Satan the ammunition to stand before God and accuse us of sin that we willfully took part in. Rev. 12:10b **For the accuser of our brothers and sisters, who accuses them before our God day and night, has been hurled down.** What we want in our lives is the declaration from the Lord, "Well done faithful servant!" Instead of giving Satan a legitimate sin report to shoot off his mouth about, we should be looking for the eyes of Jesus to affirm His righteousness at work within us while giving us the grace to overcome sin.

After Jesus had risen from the dead, He began the restoration of Peter's heart and affirmed the love God had for him. When Mary Magdalene and Mary the mother of James had gone to the tomb of Jesus, they met someone who said to them, Mark 16:7 **Now go and tell His disciples, including Peter, that Jesus is going ahead of you to Galilee. You will see Him there, just as He told you before He died.** Go tell my disciples and Peter to meet Me in Galilee and the healing can start. Make sure Peter knows to head in the direction of his redemption that only Jesus can provide.

We can learn from Christ's counselling that was given to Peter. Jesus went right to the crux of the matter. Love must be at the root of our relationship with the risen Christ, and what is on the Lord's agenda is the agenda we are to adopt. In Peter's case, love was established and the agenda was clear. John 21:15 **After breakfast Jesus asked Simon Peter, "Simon son of John, do you love me more than these?" "Yes, Lord," Peter replied, "you know I love you." "Then feed my lambs," Jesus told him.** For Peter, feeding the Lord's lambs was the love language that would help him grow in his love for God. The former Peter moment that brought condemnation had turned into an ah-ha love moment of clarity. Jesus had always loved Peter, even throughout Peter's denial. Jesus was demonstrating His love by giving Peter's heart the grace to fulfill what would be a life assignment in the kingdom of God.

What Peter moments are you still fretting over? What was the sinful event in your life that made you feel like you could never come back to believing the love God has for you? We need to remember that Christ rose from the dead so that we could be free of all the sins the devil has accused us of for decades. Like Peter, we have to turn our bad moments into an ah-ha moment where we accept the forgiveness of God through Christ and get on with the calling in our lives. We need to believe in the love that God has for us. 1John 4:16a **And we have come to know and to believe the love that God has for us**.

When we repent of our sins, that is not when God found out about them, that is when we get rid of them through the Lord's love and mercy. The power that is in the righteous blood of our Lord Jesus will take away our sin and reproach that envelops our hearts. This amazing salvation is continually working within us every moment of the day. All we have to do is rest in it and believe it by faith. People are always chasing happiness. True happiness is walking in God's forgiveness. Psalm 32:1 **O the happiness of him whose transgression is forgiven, Whose sin is covered**. Happy is that man!

Norm Sawyer

I'M THE WRONG FISHERMAN

Proverbs 1:5 Let the wise hear and increase in learning, and the one who understands obtain guidance.

I was talking with my friend Trent, and he was expressing his concern about being asked to do something ministerial that was not within his spiritual giftings. He said, "I'm the wrong fisherman for what they are asking me to do, but if they can't get anyone, I reckon I will do it until they find the right fisherman." Knowing our place in the kingdom of God is a blessing to the heart, and peace to the mind. Knowing that God has our life's plan in His hand, and has put within us certain giftings for particular work in His realm is reassuring. Jer. 29:11 **For I know the plans I have for you," declares the LORD, "plans to prosper you and not to harm you, plans to give you hope and a future.**

Being the wrong fisherman for the work at hand can be arduous to get the things that need to be accomplished done right. Having someone who cannot sing lead the congregation in the singing of praise can be hard for people to sing along without noticing the off notes and pitch. Yes, there are times when God's anointing takes over and it does not matter that the person leading is two beats behind and three notes too high, but that is God's grace loving on everyone while rescuing the time of praise and worship. It is not an endorsement that the terrible singer should keep the position. God's giftings are for specific purposes. 1Chron. 15:22 **Kenaniah the head Levite was in charge of the singing; that was his responsibility because he was skillful at it**.

I remember a brother in the Lord had been asked to lead a bible college for a couple of trimesters until a leader could be found. He accepted the position, but he was not able to fulfill what God had put in his heart under the restrictions of college leadership requirements. I could tell he was not at peace with the assignment that came to him from a committee. He looked like he was smothering in a too-tight shirt collar that was buttoned to the neck. He decided to ask God for guidance and soon his answer came, allowing him to resign from the position. Prov. 1:5 **Let the wise hear and increase in learning, and the one who understands obtain guidance.** His joy of the Lord returned in full when he was doing what God had put in his heart. As for the college position, he was the wrong fisherman for that kind of fishing in those kinds of waters.

People who know their God and know their place in His work are blessed because some people have difficulty finding their purpose and end up thinking God does not want to use them. This is so far from the truth. There are multiple areas of life where just passing a blessing forward can become a miracle in a person's life. Although most ministerial callings are exercised and developed within a church organization, not all ministry is found in a church. Most of the miracles recorded in the New Testament were done in the marketplace where common society lived their lives. People sometimes mix up the calling of God with being available in serving God. Everyone can be used by God, whether in full-time ministry or not. 2Tim. 2:20 **In a wealthy home some utensils are made of gold and silver, and some are made of wood and clay. The expensive utensils are used for special occasions, and the cheap ones are for everyday use.**

I do not mind being a cheaper vessel used for everyday use, because the fruit can be so rewarding. I was working out at the gym and noticed a young man who had not been coming as regularly. He explained that he had started Chemotherapy and didn't have the strength to work out, but decided to work out anyway. Right there at the gym, we prayed to our Heavenly Father for healing and favour during this difficult time. I was the right fisherman for that moment. James 5:16 **Confess your trespasses to one another, and pray for one another, that you may be healed. The effective, fervent prayer of a righteous man avails much**. I did not need to get permission to do what God has already asked us to do, and that is to pray for each other.

Somehow, we have made being a hand extended or a fisherman for the task on God's behalf a difficult thing. All we have to be is available, and God will move us into the right place and time. I know that we cannot die on every cross because there are so many needs to be met, but we can encourage and support those who are working tough, demanding, and burdensome ministries in God's realm. We may not feel the same compassion and have the same drive as some people, however, we can uphold them to our God so that He gives them the ability to complete their purpose. Matt. 9:38 **Therefore pray earnestly to the Lord of the harvest to send out workers into His harvest**. When we pray for others to succeed, we too are blessed in what they do.

For many of the offices in ministry, I am the wrong fisherman. If I find myself in that situation, then I need to ask God to lead me back to the waters where I do my best fishing for His kingdom. When I am fishing in the right waters, I can count on my Lord to equip me for the work. After all, the battle does belong to our Heavenly Father, and we serve our God to fulfill His vision for the world. May God bless us all and help us catch the souls He wants to bring into His realm of righteousness. Amen!

PART TWO:

QUESTIONS FOR UNDERSTANDING

1. *What did you learn in this section of the book?*
2. *What surprised you the most?*
3. *What subject(s) spoke to your heart?*
4. *Did the material that you read help you understand the subject(s) more or less?*
5. *What topics are important to you? Why?*
6. *How do these articles relate to you?*
7. *After reading this section of the book, what will you change in your life?*

PART THREE:

TRY AGAIN

Stop Watering Dead Plants

Every year the wild grass comes back and grows again. It does this because God has given the grass seeds the ability to sprout and grow for a new season. God gives us the ability to get up and try again. We may have failed for a season in our lives, but the victory is in us because Christ is in us to try again.

LOCK STOCK AND BARREL

Proverbs 31:9 Open thy mouth, judge righteously, and plead the cause of the poor and needy.

When we use the expression, "Lock, stock, and barrel," we are referring to the ownership of the whole thing or the whole enterprise. Isn't it wonderful that Jesus paid for our souls in full? He paid for us lock, stock, and barrel when He paid for our whole lives with His own life. We have been bought by the Lord, through His life-giving sacrifice that was accepted by God the Father. 1Cor. 6:20 **For you were bought at a price; therefore glorify God in your body and in your spirit, which are God's.** When we accepted Jesus as our Lord, we gave Him ownership and authority of ourselves for His eternal plan and our eternal purpose.

After man had fallen because of sin, Satan went on a rampage looking for souls to manipulate and destroy. 1Pet. 5:8 **Be sober-minded, be alert. Your adversary the devil is prowling around like a roaring lion, looking for anyone he can devour.** Fortunately for us, God had put into motion a salvation plan that would take us out of the enemy's camp and restore us to our rightful place with the Lord. God had promised that someone would come and crush the devil's authority, which he had usurped by deceiving man into sinning against God. Gen. 3:15b **He will crush your head, and you will strike his heel.** This mystery was hidden in Christ. God had a plan to get us back lock, stock, and barrel.

There truly is no peace for the wicked. Isa. 57:21 **"There is no peace," says my God, "for the wicked."** Until the resurrection of Christ, the devil spent so much of his time looking for the promised savior. Somehow or someway, Satan wanted to spoil the coming of the redeemer. The devil was always looking over his shoulder for the prophetic promise. Job 1:7 **"Where have you come from?" the LORD asked Satan. Satan answered the LORD, "I have been patrolling the earth, watching everything that's going on."** I think this might be one of the reasons why the devil had taken notice of Job. He had seen first hand that Job was protected with a hedge from God. The devil has no revelation knowledge, therefore, his thoughts might have been, "Is this the man who will crush my head?" Subsequently, Satan went after Job with an aggressive hatred.

Until the day John the Baptizer proclaimed and

spoke these words over Jesus, "Behold the lamb of God who takes away the sins of the world," Satan had no clue who he was looking for. Little did the devil know that God's redemption plan for mankind was to save us from eternal death. God's plan was also designed to destroy the works of the devil forever. Jesus had to claim us for Himself and plead our cause for our eternity. Therefore, Jesus died for our souls and got us back lock, stock, and barrel. Prov. 31:9 **Open thy mouth, judge righteously, and plead the cause of the poor and needy.**

The best part about being owned by God is that we too have ownership in all that God has for us through Christ. Those who are in Christ are heirs of what Jesus has. John 17:22 **I have given them the glory you have given me, so that they may be one as we are one. 23 I am in them and you are in me, so that they may be made completely one, that the world may know you have sent me and have loved them as you have loved me.** To be loved by God as equally as God Loves Jesus is a concept so hard to grasp, but nonetheless, it is true. Praise the Lord! Count me in!

The Apostle Paul said that everything he personally owned was rubbish compared to being owned by Christ. Phil. 3:8 **Indeed, I count**

everything as loss because of the surpassing worth of knowing Christ Jesus my Lord. For his sake I have suffered the loss of all things and count them as rubbish, in order that I may gain Christ. When we give ourselves fully to Jesus, we become lovingly owned by our heavenly Father. There is nothing better than being loved by God lock, stock, and barrel. There is nothing missing in God's love. It is fully given to us and ours to receive freely. What an amazing Lord we serve. We are entirely His through faith in Christ. Amen.

Norm Sawyer

THEN THEY WERE GONE

Proverbs 5:11 And at the end of your life you will groan when your flesh and your body are wasted away.

I have been thinking of people who influenced me during my life and who are no longer here. They have moved on to different parts of the world or passed on to their eternal rewards. They are no longer here to dispense and offer their friendship or give their timely wisdom I once gleaned from them. I find myself saying, "I had a good relationship with them and then they were gone."

They left part of themselves within my psyche and I project some of their knowledge and philosophy through my own life filters, but they are gone. We will meet again one day in the presence of the Lord, but here and now there is a vacuum where they once walked with me and spoke into my life with clear, factual, and sound wisdom for living a good and righteous life.

When someone important in our life moves on to another part of the world or passes away from this life, we can become unsettled and bewildered. The part of our life they were propping up, so to speak, tends to feel like it is drooping to the ground and exercise is needed to strengthen that part of our life. Every person created has to deal with this type of loss during their short time on earth. We are temporal beings, after all, and one day it will be said of us, "Then they were gone." James 4:14 **You do not even know what will happen tomorrow! What is your life? You are a mist that appears for a little while and then vanishes.**

Sometimes God moves these people out of our lives. The skills these people had and we became dependent on were good for a while but now it is time for us to mature, man-up or take the responsibility for our part in God's great plan. Psalm 32:8 **I will instruct you and teach you in the way you should go; I will counsel you with my loving eye on you.** We will always be grateful to those who taught us and helped us through that portion of our life, but the time comes when we have to take the reins God gave us. John 16:13a **When the Spirit of truth comes, he will guide you into all the truth.**

If there was ever a hard time for a man to step up and take the reins of life and leadership, it is when Joshua had to take over when Moses had been taken by God. Now those were big boots to fill and a gigantic step of faith that had to take place in Joshua's heart to become the next visionary and leader. I am sure Joshua said on a few occasions: "Now what do I do? Moses is gone." Joshua, like everyone else in life, needed direction and encouragement from God as to what to do next. Josh. 1:2 **Moses My servant is dead. Now therefore, arise, go over this Jordan, you and all this people, to the land which I am giving to them—the children of Israel.**

Does the Lord move these mentors out of our lives to make us depend on God more than we have been doing? Josh. 1:9 **Have I not commanded you? Be strong and of good courage; do not be afraid, nor be dismayed, for the LORD your God is with you wherever you go.** Joshua, like us all, needed that word of the Lord to accelerate him toward his destiny written by God. I am sure there were times when Joshua and Caleb said to themselves: "Then they were gone and we have to step up and do it." However, they became legends in life and a blessing to their generation.

I write these thoughts in memory and gratitude of all the people throughout my life who have given me good and honest insight into living a worthwhile life. I might sound like I'm at a podium, the recipient of some award listing all the people who made my life possible and victorious. Maybe there should be a list written up and then prayed over, giving thanks to God for His goodness toward all the great people He brought into my life for the growth I needed. This might be a good idea because inevitably we will all look back one day and realize they are gone. Hopefully, they will be blessed with what we did with the impute they gave us for a God-like life. To everyone who has blessed me with their friendship, I say: "Thank You."

WHY?

Proverbs 25:2 It is the glory of God to conceal a thing: but the honour of kings is to search out a matter.

Why, why, why? This question is asked in some cases all day long. Why God? Why is this happening to me? What did I do to deserve this? Why is it not turning out the way I thought? A few days ago I heard a response to the question "Why?" Someone asked, "Why did this happen to me?" The person answering simply said, "I don't know, I can't answer that question." The answer was the truth, he could not even begin to answer a question that only God could answer.

Now it was my turn. I asked God, in my mind, why was there no answer in the natural for this person. I started laughing within myself because I was doing the same thing - asking why. I know in my heart there are scriptures that say I can ask and I will receive. Matt. 7:7 **Ask, and it shall be given you; seek, and ye shall find; knock, and it shall be opened unto you:** 8 **For every one that asks receives; and he that seeks finds;**

and to him that knocks it shall be opened.

Other scriptures admonish us to ask God for wisdom for our lives. James 1:5 **If any of you lacks wisdom, you should ask God, who gives generously to all without finding fault, and it will be given to you.** With God encouraging us to ask Him for wisdom and answers that only God can answer, why are we left wanting answers? What is missing in the way we are asking that leaves us apparently without answers?

We read in the book of Genesis the story of Abraham who had been given a promise that Sarah would give birth to a child fathered by Abraham and fulfill the plan of God. Gen. 17:16 **And I will bless her, and give thee a son also of her: yea, I will bless her, and she shall be a mother of nations; kings of people shall be of her.** Now Abraham is being given this promise from God. For some reason, Abraham starts asking God if the plan could be changed and Ishmael might be used instead of what God has stated and wants. Gen. 17:18 **And Abraham said unto God, O that Ishmael might live before thee!**

Abraham is basically saying, "Why can't we do it my way?" God responds by saying, "It will be done my way since I am God and you are not and I see all the blessings in the future from this covenant." Gen. 17:21 **But my covenant will I**

establish with Isaac, which Sarah shall bear unto thee at this set time in the next year. As I read this I thought of all the "Why Lord can't you do it my way?" The question comes out of us so easily. However, the result ends up with us standing there saying, "Why, why, why?"

What we have to understand is that God understands our dilemmas, feelings, and being in a state of total questioning. As Joyce Meyer said, "Grace is not opposed to us making an effort toward victory." We are trying to get the answers for victory in our lives, but we have to keep on the plan that God has for us in His Kingdom. Jesus Himself had to overcome the same feelings we feel. Luke 22:42 **Saying, Father, if thou be willing, remove this cup from me: nevertheless not my will, but thine, be done.**

There would be a lot less - Why Lord? - if we stuck to the original instruction our hearts received from God the first time He spoke to us by His Spirit. Like Jesus, we have to come to that place where we are saying, "Not my will, but your will be done, Lord." Jer. 29:13 **And ye shall seek me, and find me, when ye shall search for me with all your heart.**

We have been given the grace by God to seek out a matter as the Proverb says. We have also been given an instruction to believe God is trustworthy and truthful toward us by what we see in Jesus. John 14:11 **Believe me that I am in the Father, and the Father in me: or else believe me for the very works' sake.**

The answer that Jesus had for every question was always the will of the Father and Christ would manifest that will from healing to provision and satisfactory answers for the soul. Do I continue to ask why? Absolutely, but I try to ask in sincerity of heart because it seems to be the only way I have peace when I am asking, "Why Lord?" Eph. 6:24 **Grace be with all them that love our Lord Jesus Christ in sincerity.** Amen.

Norm Sawyer

BROKEN? FIX IT!

Proverbs 29:1 One who becomes stiff-necked, after many reprimands will be shattered instantly—beyond recovery.

What a strange couple of weeks I have had. All kinds of little things kept breaking that needed repair or fixing right away. We got about a foot of snow one day and the snow blower would not start. A tiny metal fiber had plugged up a small part of the carburetor. The wipers on my car stopped in mid-wipe and needed fixing. The glove compartment latch snapped off and a band-aid repair was needed to stop everything from falling out onto the car floor. The toilet started a small leak at the floor and a new wax ring was needed. I dropped my electric toothbrush on the floor and it stopped buzzing away. It had been a gift. It had to be fixed. Then a few days ago the hood support stabilizers of my car would not keep the hood up. It let out a grinding noise and that was it.

Outside of the fact that the little breakdowns kept me busy figuring out what had to be done, there was nothing really dramatic here because all of these little annoyances could be repaired or fixed. The only odd thing was that these things kept happening one after another, therefore, it was noticeable. If these things are happening in the natural, what is going on in the spirit?

How many little things are breaking down or malfunctioning in our soul that God has talked to us about that need fixing? Why have we not asked the Lord for help in fixing the sinful things that we fall for so easily? If God says something is not right within us, then we should be on it. With God's help and grace, we should be repenting, restoring, and repairing the wrong taking place within us. Phil. 2:12 **Therefore, my dear friends, just as you have always obeyed, so now, not only in my presence but even more in my absence, work out your own salvation with fear and trembling.**

We can become accustomed to living with broken appliances, furniture, vehicles and putting up with a patchwork of fixes that will get by for now. This attitude does not work in the kingdom of God. Nor should it. God is perfect and desires obedience. When He asks us to do His will, He doesn't expect us to say, "Ya well, I'll get around to it sometime soon." We do not bring God down to our level of procrastination, but rather we rise to His level of perfection that He may be glorified and we may live and be blessed.

The danger in being lackadaisical with God's directions in our life is that we may end up not caring or doing what He asks of us. Disobedient people will get to the point where they no longer listen to the Holy Spirit and their stiffneckedness will put them in a precarious position to be destroyed by the enemy of their soul. Prov. 6:15 **Therefore calamity will come upon him suddenly; in a moment he will be broken beyond healing.** All because they did not obey the first simple instruction that was doable at the time. However, now they have become rebels because they did not fix the small things that were pointed out in love by God. 1Sam 15:23 **For rebellion is as the sin of witchcraft, and stubbornness is as iniquity and idolatry. Because thou hast rejected the word of the LORD, he hath also rejected thee from being king.**

It is simple, saints. In the same way, when we come across something needing repair at home or work, we get on it and do it. When God points out sin or problem, then we get on it and allow the Lord to fix it with our volition and cooperation. God will take notice, and He will help us if we ask for His help. Psalm 46:1 **God is our refuge and strength, a very present help in trouble.**

We were created to solve problems. How

much more could we do if we asked the God of all knowledge and wisdom for help? Broken? Fix it! Father, in Jesus name, help us not be afraid to ask you for all the help we need every day of our lives. Amen and amen!

TIME TO DREAM AGAIN

Proverbs 16:9 A man's heart devises his way: but the LORD directs his steps.

"No person has the right to rain on your dreams." Martin Luther King Jr.

What have we put on hold because we were struck down with some life event that was out of our control? What have we stopped dreaming about that used to make us so happy when we mused on the thought of its possibilities? Have you stopped dreaming?

God has put dreams within us that are only ours because they came from God in the first place. He created us with the ability to dream and know we could be part of their creation and realization. God's dreams within us is a language from the Holy. God is right there beside us, dreaming along with us and hoping we put our trust in Him to bring it to pass. Heb. 11:8 **By faith Abraham, when he was called to go out into a place which he should after receive for an inheritance, obeyed; and he went out, not knowing whither he went. 9 By faith he** sojourned in the land of promise, as in a strange country, dwelling in tabernacles with Isaac and Jacob, the heirs with him of the same promise: 10 For he looked for a city which hath foundations, whose builder and maker is God.

Our dreams in God are possible when we move with the Holy Spirit to accomplish them. I like what Jesse Duplantis says, "Believe the unbelievable and receive the impossible." Why should we start dreaming again? If we don't, we will fade out. Prov. 29:18a **Where there is no vision, the people perish.**

Dreaming keeps us alive and looking forward for the miracle in our lives. Dreaming keeps our hearts coming to God for answers for the accomplishments of our goals. Dreaming gives us new life and brings forth new ideas that keep us moving toward an expected result. Prov. 23:18 **For surely there is a result, and thine expectation shall not be cut off.** Oh yeah. Dreaming is free; it costs nothing.

Solomon was dreaming, envisioning and thinking of having the ability to take care of a nation and interestingly God comes to him in a dream. Go figure! 1Kings 3:5 **In Gibeon the LORD appeared to Solomon in a dream by night: and God said, Ask what I shall give**

thee. Solomon comes right out and says what he wants and what he requires to fulfill what he has been dreaming about. 1Kings 3:9 **Give therefore thy servant an understanding heart to judge thy people, that I may discern between good and bad: for who is able to judge this thy so great a people? 10 And the speech pleased the Lord, that Solomon had asked this thing.** We know that Solomon got what he asked for as the wisdom of Solomon is established from that day on.

We are so fortunate to live in the dispensation of the New Testament because dreams, visions and dreaming is a promise of the Holy Spirit for those of us who are in Christ. Joel 2:28 **And it shall come to pass afterward, that I will pour out my spirit upon all flesh; and your sons and your daughters shall prophesy, your old men shall dream dreams, your young men shall see visions: 29 And also upon the servants and upon the handmaids in those days will I pour out my spirit.**

Since this Scripture belongs to us, then we should go for it and dream away. Let's put our thoughts of the heart out there where God can see them and help us tweak them so they become part of the building of the kingdom of God. Share your heart with the Lord and show Him the deep desires that you have. The Lord is a gentleman and will not mock your dreaming. He might even show you how to make them come to pass.

You may have been dreaming the same thing for years and there does not seem to be a way to get there. Maybe you have been struck with a terminal illness and your dreams have been put on hold. You might have suffered a great financial bankruptcy and your dreams seem so far out of reach. Perhaps the ones you once dreamed with have passed away and you do not know how to go on with the dream that was once a joy but now has turned to sadness.

God had a dream for us all and He made sure it came to pass for us through the work of the cross and the cleansing blood of the Lord Jesus. Surely if God went to that extent to show us His perfect love, will He not come alongside our heart's desires and dreams to accomplish that which He created for us and in us? Yes, Saints, it is time to dream again and with a voice of victory declare the promises of God in our dreams. Call upon the name of the Lord, because He will answer us. Jer. 33:3 **Call unto me, and I will answer thee, and shew thee great and mighty things, which thou know not.** Sweet dreams Saints.

Huummmmmmmmmmmmmm

Proverbs 4:11 I have taught thee in the way of wisdom; I have led thee in right paths.

Lately, some people I know in the workplace have been encouraging me to meditate. I need to empty my mind and just not think about anything others say. This will do me some real good. I explained to them that I do meditate on the word of God. They say, "That is not clearing your mind and you need to be more open-minded and venture out from the word of God only."

They say "You need to allow other influences into your spirit so that you can be elevated to a new reality. Test the other things, other than your narrow ideas of God." No, I don't think so. I like my relationship with my God and Saviour. God's thoughts toward me are to do me good.

I don't think that is what God meant when He asks us to meditate on Him and His word. God seems very clear that we are to meditate on Him and his word regularly. The word of God encourages us to meditate in the word of God and on the works of His hands. Psalm 119:148

Mine eyes prevent the night watches, that I might meditate in thy word. Psalm 77:12 **I will meditate also of all thy work, and talk of thy doings.**

As a matter of fact, God told Joshua the answer to his success was that he should meditate on the law of God day and night. Josh. 1:8 **This book of the law shall not depart out of thy mouth; but thou shalt meditate therein day and night, that thou may observe to do according to all that is written therein: for then thou shalt make thy way prosperous, and then thou shalt have good success.**

Paul admonished Timothy to meditate on the things that had been prophesied over him by the word of God. 1Tim. 4:15 **Meditate upon these things; give thyself wholly to them; that thy profiting may appear to all. 16 Take heed unto thyself, and unto the doctrine; continue in them: for in doing this thou shalt both save thyself, and them that hear thee.**

We read in the book of Judges the problem with mixing in the smorgasbord of other beliefs with the foundational truth of God being the only God. After the death of Joshua and the elders who had seen the miracles of God's deliverance of Israel into the promised land. There started to be a problem with the next generation. Judg. 2:10

And also all that generation were gathered unto their fathers: and there arose another generation after them, which knew not the LORD, nor yet the works which He had done for Israel.11 **And the children of Israel did evil in the sight of the LORD, and served Baalim:** 12 **And they forsook the LORD God of their fathers, which brought them out of the land of Egypt, and followed other gods, of the gods of the people that were round about them, and bowed themselves unto them, and provoked the LORD to anger.**

The next generation had not learned how to meditate on the law of God for success because they were living the dream per-se. They had become comfortable with their surroundings and social standing that expressed, "Live and let live." So what if there were still Canaanites, Jebusites, Asherites, Amorites, and the Philistines influencing how Israel should worship. After it is all said and done, all roads lead to the same god.

Well, God did not think this to be true. Ex. 20:2 **I am the LORD thy God, which have brought thee out of the land of Egypt, out of the house of bondage.** 3 **Thou shalt have no other gods before me.** The problem Israel had with falling for other gods is that they ended up eating the fruit of the other gods. Judg. 2:19b

They ceased not from their own doings, nor from their stubborn way. 20a And the anger of the LORD was hot against Israel. 21 I also will not henceforth drive out any from before them of the nations which Joshua left when he died. They could have had a great relationship with the All Mighty God but they ended up with the common everyday detritus of a dime a dozen gods.

What has the world asked us to meditate on lately? Fear of the future. Lack of supply, ending up in starvation. Sickness and disease in old age. Wars and devastation for our children. No, saints! That is not why God wants us to meditate on His word and His ways. God wants His wisdom to be our thought life and therefore our prayer life will declare the wishes and desires of our God into this lost world.

We are the salt and light of this world because we meditate on the life giver. No, friends, I would not trade that for a mantra. No, not ever. Phil. 4:8 **Finally, brethren, whatsoever things are true, whatsoever things are honest, whatsoever things are just, whatsoever things are pure, whatsoever things are lovely, whatsoever things are of good report; if there be any virtue, and if there be any praise, think on these things.** Blessings and prosperity to you all.

SERIOUSLY?

Proverbs 11:4 Riches profit not in the day of wrath: but righteousness delivers from death.

Someone said, "The difference between try and triumph, is the umph!"

What have we been trying to overcome in our lives that we know will make a difference in our relationship with God? If we could just get over that umph that is hindering us, what would our God-walk look like? We apply so much focus on the problem that we have not stopped to ask God for the help that will actually work in our victory. It seems as though God is the last person we go to for help when trying to get closer to Him.

Seriously, why is that? We spend all kinds of time, money, and energy on things that will give us free time and so-called rest so that we can spend time with God. Meanwhile, the Lord is saying in His word that He will give us the rest we actually need. Matt.11:28 **Come unto me, all ye that labour and are heavy laden, and I will give you rest.** However, we have to do it the Lord's way and in this case it is "Come to me," says the

Lord.

We are trying to get to God with our own logic and interpretations. It is Christ's righteousness that gets us into a relationship with God and not our own doing. It has to be that way because God is righteous and functions from that position. If it were left up to man we would end up trying to buy, bribe, cajole and steal the favor of God with different antics and activities.

The results of this human attempt for relationship with God would be a hodge-podge of dead works that look like filthy rags. Isa. 64:6 **But we are all as an unclean thing, and all our righteousnesses are as filthy rags; and we all do fade as a leaf; and our iniquities, like the wind, have taken us away.** It's not that man is not sincere in his attempt to reach God, but man cannot see what is needed from God's point of view and thus wisdom vanishes from man's heart. Just look around the world and you will see no lack of stupidity.

I was listening to a story about a smoker who was complaining that his doctor wanted him to quit smoking because the beginning of emphysema had started in his body. Seriously? He was complaining that he should stop smoking because it was killing him.

I wondered if I was that thick when asking

God for help as the Lord stated the clear and obvious solution out to me. Seriously? Do I complain to God for the fact that He is trying to save my life? Mal. 3:13a **"Your words have been harsh against Me," Says the LORD.** Yes, Lord. Forgive me for my arrogance and presumption toward you. You are Lord! Righteousness delivers from death and you are righteous.

We read the story of Simon the Sorcerer who thought God could be bought. Acts 8:9 **But there was a certain man called Simon, who previously practiced sorcery in the city and astonished the people of Samaria, claiming that he was someone great, 10 to whom they all gave heed, from the least to the greatest, saying, "This man is the great power of God."**

The apostles were preaching Christ crucified and laying hands on the people that they would be baptized in the Holy Spirit. When Simon saw this miracle taking place, he asked the apostles if he could buy from them the power that did this great work. Acts 8:18 **And when Simon saw that through laying on of the apostles' hands the Holy Ghost was given, he offered them money, 19 Saying, Give me also this power, that on whomsoever I lay hands, he may receive the Holy Ghost.**

The answer that Peter gives is stern and to the point. God cannot be bought! There has to be a heart transplant per-se to be in a relationship with him. Acts 8:20 **But Peter said unto him, Thy money perish with thee, because thou hast thought that the gift of God may be purchased with money. 21 Thou hast neither part nor lot in this matter: for thy heart is not right in the sight of God**. As you can see, if left up to man the approach to God is corrupt and devious.

Seriously Simon, you want to buy the Holy Spirit? Seeking God is our privilege, because we are human, but we are to seek and find Him God's way. There is nothing wrong with putting a bit of umph into our seeking and loving of God. Let us proceed with God's way of doing things and bring about the Kingdom of God and its fullness.

The first step has been made for us; we just have to believe it and live it by faith. Rom.10:8 **But what saith it? The word is nigh thee, even in thy mouth, and in thy heart: that is, the word of faith, which we preach; 9 That if thou shalt confess with thy mouth the Lord Jesus, and shalt believe in thine heart that God hath raised him from the dead, thou shalt be saved.** Seriously, it is that simple.

GOD ALSO LOVES ATHEISTS

Proverbs 6:9 But you, lazybones, how long will you sleep? When will you wake up?

Atheists do not exist because God does not believe in them.

I find it humorous when someone says they are making a decision as to whether or not to make Jesus the Lord of their life. I always want to jump in and say, "Jesus is already Lord! You are simply accepting the fact of this reality by submitting to His Lordship that was eternally established from the beginning of time." 1Pet. 1:20 **He was chosen before the creation of the world, but was revealed in these last times for your sake.**

We have people who claim to be agnostic and feel they can keep their distance from God because they do not believe it is possible to have a relationship with a divine God. An atheist comes along and dribbles out some psychobabble about nothing because there is nothing to believe in and so on it goes. What is it about the human condition that is always testing the love of God? Why do we have to be so stubborn?

We have come through hundreds of years of so-called enlightenment and can barely see how to get along with our neighbours. We claim to have gained deep insight into life's mysteries and can hardly understand our own emotions on the surface, let alone deep ones. We keep missing the spiritual because we keep looking for an intuitive worldly answer. Spiritual things must be spiritually discerned. 1Cor. 2:14 **The person without the Spirit does not accept the things that come from the Spirit of God but considers them foolishness, and cannot understand them because they are discerned only through the Spirit.**

The Apostle Paul was having to think through similar and established beliefs when he was trying to get through to the Corinthian mindset because they were trying to cover all the basis for all types of lifestyle choices by having ready-made gods available to cover any whim and circumstance. The people of the day had set up many gods so they could be petitioned for any possible event. Within their cluster of gods to choose from, they even had one named *the unknown god*. Acts 17:23 **For as I passed along and observed the objects of your worship, I found also an altar with this inscription, 'To the unknown god.' What therefore you worship as unknown, this**

I proclaim to you.

It was thought that by offering a spiritual smorgasbord of gods they could cover their lifestyle choices regardless of what their choices were. It looks to me like not much has changed since that time. Eccl. 1:9 **What has been will be again, what has been done will be done again; there is nothing new under the sun.**

People, in our time and history, are still trying to make their gods work for them by self-pronounced validation of their life choices regardless of what the Almighty God has said about it. Within churches, we have people rewriting and reinterpreting clearly spelled out scriptures to suit their own sin of choice.

At this point, I will be accused by some of not having an open mind because of what I have just implied. Our minds should not be so open that our brains are falling out. Righteousness is righteousness and sin is sin! Isa. 5:20 **Woe to those who call evil good and good evil, who put darkness for light and light for darkness, who put bitter for sweet and sweet for bitter.**

It is God who tells us to be reconciled to Himself and not a suggestion as to whether we want to or not. It is a divine instruction to do so. 2Cor. 5:18 **All this is from God, who reconciled us to himself through Christ and gave us the** ministry of reconciliation: 19 **that God was reconciling the world to himself in Christ, not counting people's sins against them. And he has committed to us the message of reconciliation.**

You may not believe God exists or you may believe that you cannot have a divine relationship with Him, but this does not eliminate our personal invitation from God to accept His loving gift of salvation through Christ the Lord. You may have rejected God's eternal offer, but you have been served with His edict of love. Titus 2:11 **For the grace of God that brings salvation hath appeared to all men,** 12 **teaching us that, denying ungodliness and worldly lusts, we should live soberly, righteously, and godly, in this present world.**

Atheism, agnosticism, and every other humanism is not enlightenment. It is the belief of believing in nothing which is creating empty souls and resulting in a generation of spiritual sloths. Christ describes these so-called teachers of nothingness; the blind leading the blind. Matt. 15:14 **Let them alone: they be blind leaders of the blind. And if the blind lead the blind, both shall fall into the ditch.**

God loves atheists, agnostics, and humanists alike. Christ died for every person ever created.

God believes in you. If He did not believe in you, He would not have created you. God knows our eternal potential and purpose, so why would we hand our created purpose over to some self-proclaimed Antichrist or a teacher of emptiness?

No, it's time to wake up from the sleep of the slothful. Jesus is Lord of all and every knee will bow to that fact. We can bow now and live in the joy of the Lord, or bow on the other side of death and weep. Either way, we will all bow to the Lordship of Jesus. Phil. 2:10 **That at the name of Jesus every knee should bow, in the heavens and on earth and under the earth.** Jesus is Lord!

ONE WAY TICKET

Proverbs 12:28 In the way of righteousness there is life; along that path is immortality.

I heard someone say, "Wherever time goes it takes your life with it."

We have all been given a one-way ticket in this life. We move forward with time creating our own history. There is no way back to our youth, or even to yesterday evening. It is done and gone. What we do have is the present moment in our existence, and what we put our heart into at this moment will determine our future. Psalm 118:24 **This is the day the LORD has made. We will rejoice and be glad in it.**

We think we are in control of our future, but this is an illusion we fool ourselves with. We cannot predict anything for sure as life and living is fleeting and without guarantees. James 4:14 **Whereas you don't know what your life will be like tomorrow. For what is your life? For you are a vapor, that appears for a little time, and then vanishes away.** Our one-way ticket was punched from the first day we took the first breath on this earth. It will only take us as far as God has determined it will. We can go kicking and screaming or we can go in peace, but we're going forward toward our eternity with or without God; this is our choice and free will.

For those of us who are going forward with God, we have been given additional blessings to help us along the way of life's journey. Our ticket has been bumped up to heaven class, so to speak, as the blessings of God's promises have been given and made to us who are in Christ. 2Pet. 1:4 **And because of his glory and excellence, he has given us great and precious promises. These are the promises that enable you to share his divine nature and escape the world's corruption caused by human desires.**

Jesus is the author and finisher of our faith. Heb. 12:2a **Looking unto Jesus the author and finisher of our faith.** The only thing in life we have control over is whether we give full control of our soul to our savior and let Him direct the path of our life and immortality. Prov. 12:28 **In the way of righteousness there is life; along that path is immortality.** The choice is truly ours to make. We decide whether to go with God, or we go with ourselves on our own. Eze. 21:16 **Cut sharply to the right; set yourself to the left, wherever your face is directed.**

Stop Watering Dead Plants

Time waits for no man. Time doesn't even wait for time. We are on the track of life and our motion and momentum picks up and moves faster every day toward our eternal station. I often hear people saying, "Enjoy the ride." I have to agree in this case, because this life is the only one we have. Let us fill our life with joy and hope so that our travels are blessed and fulfilling. Let God be our guide through all the difficulties life can hand out. Let us take part in all the blessings that God has for us, so when we get to our eternal destination we are whole and full of the spirit of God.

I don't know where time goes, but I know where I am going. I'm traveling with the King of kings and the Lord of lords toward a love-filled eternity Christ gave me. I press toward the promises God has given me through Jesus and I live in the here and now with Him. Phil. 3:14 **I press on toward the goal to win the prize of God's heavenly calling in Christ Jesus.**

OUR DISHONORABLE HONORABLES

Proverbs 18:12 Before his downfall a person's heart is proud, but humility comes before honor..

Numbers 32:23 **But if you don't do this, you will certainly sin against the LORD; be sure your sin will catch up with you.**

There have been some nasty fallouts within all political stripes and parties this year in federal and provincial politics. Accusations of past indiscretions, sexual misconduct, and inappropriate behavior has come out of the closet in full force. Our honorable members of parliament have found themselves on display, 'fessing up to dishonorable life choices they made within their elected positions.' One of the members who has expressed shame and disappointment said, "No wonder the people hate politicians, because all they see are a bunch of crooks and creeps!"

I do believe there are a lot of members of Parliament who truly try and are doing their best to make things better for the people they represent. God wants good government because He asks us to uphold the law. Rom. 13:1 **Let everyone be subject to the governing authorities, for there is no authority except that which God has established. The authorities that exist have been established by God.**

It is hard to be forthright and pure in the eyes of the public when these members live in a fishbowl, so to speak, where everyone on earth has an eye on them and a ready opinion of their lives and character. I know I would not want the job because I am not always so politically correct. So, therefore, I have to take up the call God expects of me and that is to pray for our leaders. 1Tim. 2:2 **Pray this way for kings and all who are in authority so that we can live peaceful and quiet lives marked by godliness and dignity.**

We have to stop and think that if we as individuals need prayer on a daily basis to get through our week or even our work day, then how much more do these members need prayer to get through their day? I realize that the integrity bar per se has been set so low these days that people in leadership are stubbing their toe on the bar as they walk over it; therefore, anything seems to be acceptable.

The prayer we are to ask God to accomplish in these parliamentarian's lives is that the bar of ethics would be raised and followed. This can be done by faith because God can change their hearts and lead them. Prov. 21:1 **The king's heart is a stream of water in the hand of the LORD; he turns it wherever he will.** Lord, God, help them raise the bar of ethics and due diligence to a place where they see a need to rise up to greatness and become the leaders they are intended to be.

When we pray for our leaders and God moves on their hearts, there is a fruitful reward. We shall prosper as the land and leaders prosper. Jer. 29:7 **Also, seek the peace and prosperity of the city to which I have carried you into exile. Pray to the LORD for it, because if it prospers, you too will prosper.**

When we pray for our church or political leaders and ask God to move upon their hearts to help them repent and work accordingly with the wishes of God, our land and nation will be healed. 2Chron. 7:14 **If my people, who are called by my name, will humble themselves and pray and seek my face and turn from their wicked ways, then I will hear from heaven, and I will forgive their sin and will heal their land.**

It seems to me that praying for our honorable members and leaders of all kinds has nothing but upside because of all the blessings that come to us when they succeed in their calling and work.

Perhaps if more of us used our mouths for praying for our leaders rather than slandering them to death, the dishonorable ones would be weeded out by God and the honorable ones would go forth.

Maybe that is what God is showing us these days. It is God who is in charge and we need to pray that the purging going on will keep cleaning house and we can have a blessed nation. Psalm 2:10 **Therefore, you kings, be wise; be warned, you rulers of the earth. 11 Serve the LORD with fear and celebrate his rule with trembling.** Pray the dishonor out and the honor back in. Blessings.

THE JUNK DRAWER

Proverbs 8:21 That I may cause those that love me to inherit substance; and I will fill their treasures.

I can venture to say that most homes have a junk drawer and some have a few of them. I was looking for a phone number that I had written on a card and put it at the back of a small notebook. I thought the notebook was in a particular drawer and I went looking for it. Well, I found many things in that drawer but not the number. I found instruction manuals for products I no longer owned because they had worn out or been discarded. I found other numbers of people that had a long time moved away and in some cases passed away.

I found pens and markers that I thought were lost. I found photos and clippings of longtime memories past. Scratched DVDs, guitar plectrums, batteries, bits and parts of things I was not sure what they were for. Literally, everything but the kitchen sink was found in this drawer. but not the card I was looking for. I even forgot what I was looking for as I was drawn away by all the junk that had to be sorted, repurposed and thrown away. I thought of the word of God that said, " All the cares of this world enter in and choke the word." Mark 4:19 **And the cares of this world, and the deceitfulness of riches, and the lusts of other things entering in, choke the word, and it becomes unfruitful.**

All the accumulated stuff in our lives can pile up and we can become lost in the junk drawer of our being and find out there is no substance or quality items. Just a lot of junk that has to be chucked out. We sometimes go looking for an answer from God but the detritus of life is clogging up the clarity of His answer. We approach in prayer with a ready-made view of how we think God should answer the prayer and thus miss the entire blessing that He had for us. No real substance, just junk in the way of growth in life.

When I find myself in that place, I stand up like Moses and with my arms held high to the sky, I pray the prayer that never fails. Matt. 6:10 **Thy kingdom come. Thy will be done in earth, as it is in heaven.** It is one of my shortest prayers but it is the one that delivers me when I say, "Thy will be done." I know I cannot go wrong with this prayer and I know it is the will of God. I have found that this prayer is the only thing that cleans up the junk in the drawer of my life.

All the books on five steps to receiving, three steps to getting, and the four principles of having all get chucked out and replaced with the proclamation of "God's will be done." This only clears the junk out of the way. 1John 5:14 **And this is the confidence that we have in Him, that, if we ask any thing according to His will, He hears us: 15 And if we know that He hear us, whatsoever we ask, we know that we have the petitions that we desired of Him.**

What has been choking the word of God in your life lately? Is it a lot of stuff that you are trying to juggle around God's word in hopes of making everything fit and run smoothly? Where is our treasure in God? Is it in the stuff we can get from Him or in the heart of Him? Jer. 29:13 **And ye shall seek me, and find me, when ye shall search for me with all your heart.** Matt. 6:21 **For where your treasure is, there will your heart be also.**

I want the junk in my life removed and thrown away so that I can fill my being with the true substance of God's being. I want what counts in this life and not the temporary baubles the world offers at an overrated extraordinary price. Creating a habit of removing junk from our lives is a good habit. Someone said, "The chains of habit are too light to be felt until they're too heavy to be broken."

Have we become used to having a lot of junk in our lives? We have to break that habit now before we are overwhelmed with all the stuff that gets in the way of the blessing of God. I, therefore, speak a word of overcoming victory over all of us. Isa. 57:10 **You grew weary in your search, but you never gave up. Desire gave you renewed strength, and you did not grow weary**. Amen!

AM I RELEVANT?

Proverbs 26:6 He that sends a message by the hand of a fool cuts off the feet, and drinks damage.

Why are you resigning from teaching in the Bible college? "I am no longer relevant to the new wave of student," I said, in response to her question. "What do you mean by relevant? You are relevant to me," she said. "Yes, I am relevant as a person, father, husband and friend but not as a teacher teaching in this old way for these times. I am still using an older method of teaching. I am still explaining and drawing on blackboards and handing out papers with expectations of participation in the class."

I would look up from my notes and all I could see were students looking down at their communication devices and I had no idea if they were learning anything or even listening. I realized that I was no longer relevant to the modern bible college student and I had to act on this knowledge before I became a fool with a non-message with nothing to say.

We must be people who know the times we are ministering in or at least be relevant to the times, or we will become the old fool there is no fool like. 1Chron. 12:32a **And of the children of Issachar, which were men that had understanding of the times, to know what Israel ought to do.**

I remember this conversation like it was yesterday. I remember arriving at that place of mind and wondering if I was relevant to the Kingdom of God in that place and time. I was teaching the same old things in the same old ways. I started noticing a lot of the older Pastors, church-itineraries and TV ministries doing the same old thing. There were a lot of people in the pulpits with nothing to say.

There were words coming from their lips and TV screens but it was just bland regurgitated pablum coming out of these old systems and I did not want to be another minister with nothing to say. It was time to shut it down and relearn how to communicate to the new generation of app-specialists. I needed to learn how to teach all over again. Luke 12:12 **For the Holy Ghost shall teach you in the same hour what ye ought to say.**

There is nothing more pitiful and embarrassing than watching some old TV evangelist using the same old methods from the nineteen-seventies to prod this new and gadget-driven generation into becoming Christians and also a supporter of the TV ministry making the rehearsed plea. The new communicators who have a vibrant and grace-filled message are leading the way in churches today because they have something to say.

Jesus is Lord and He still saves from sin, and heals, provides and blesses the people of the earth because God loves the people in the world. John 3:16 **For God so loved the world, that he gave his only begotten Son, that whosoever believes in him should not perish, but have everlasting life.** Somehow these communicators and ministries have downloaded from the Holy Spirit an inspired word of God's love and grace that is hitting the hearts of a new generation of saints. Isa. 43:19 **Behold, I will do a new thing; now it shall spring forth; shall ye not know it? I will even make a way in the wilderness, and rivers in the desert.**

How do we remain relevant to the move of God in this day? We know that God wants us to bear fruit in old age. Psalm 92:14 **Those that be planted in the house of the LORD shall flourish in the courts of our God. 15 They shall still bring forth fruit in old age; they shall be fat and flourishing.** So, it looks like we do not have to worry about ministry retirement as we get older. We can remain relevant to the body of Christ and in our Christian lives.

We progress in relevance when we press into what God is saying and we act on it by faith. Isa. 40:31 **But they that wait upon the LORD shall renew their strength; they shall mount up with wings as eagles; they shall run, and not be weary; and they shall walk, and not faint.** We are relevant to the church body when we renew our minds in the word of God and from that heart's position become a hand extended in the Kingdom of our Lord. Eph. 4:3 **And be renewed in the spirit of your mind; 5 And that ye put on the new man, which after God is created in righteousness and true holiness.** We continue to be relevant when we hear the word of God and do it as faithful ambassadors in His Kingdom. Rom. 10:17 **So then faith comes by hearing, and hearing by the word of God.**

I believe I did relearn how to become a better teacher and communicator to the generation that has suckled off of an air of entitlement. The millennial generation who cannot live without granite countertops. Generation X and Y who are continually looking for identity participating in everything extreme. We will have to communicate a real testimony to this group of people and that will be a time of real relevance for us all.

I did not resign from teaching to quit reaching out. I retooled my teaching skills to reach out and capture the hearts of a generation that God loves and Jesus died for. The mandate of the Lord has not changed. Mark 16:15 **And He said unto them, Go ye into all the world, and preach the gospel to every creature.** However, the methods of fulfilling this mandate have changed and we must align our hearts with what God is doing. Don't be afraid to try something newly God inspired, because there is mercy for us all. Lam. 3:22 **It is of the LORD'S mercies that we are not consumed, because his compassions fail not. 23 They are new every morning: great is thy faithfulness.**

IF NOT NOW, WHEN?

Proverbs 7:24 Hearken unto me now therefore, O ye children, and attend to the words of my mouth.

I have been asking myself this question a lot: "If not now, when?" There seems to be an urgency in the Holy Spirit within me that is asking me to move forward in the maturation of God and all the blessings He has for me because of who I am in Christ. If I slow down just a bit with an exaggerated excuse as to why I want to do the assignment later on, I hear a soft nudge saying, 'If not now, when?' 2Cor. 6:2 **For he says, "In the time of my favor I heard you, and in the day of salvation I helped you." I tell you, now is the time of God's favor, now is the day of salvation.**

Putting off the inevitable lesson God is trying to get through to us is a mug's game. There is no way around the growing process in the eternal plan of God. The Lord will build His church with or without us. That would be such a sad moment in any Christian's life to be left out of the greatest holy project in the universe, because we are the church body of Christ. So, why would we hinder our growth? We are either for God working within us or against His righteous guidance. There is no middle ground of lukewarmness. Rev. 3:15 **I know your deeds, that you are neither cold nor hot. I wish you were either one or the other!**

The love God has for us is helping us move forward to a place where we are ever growing into the image of Christ. When I look in the mirror, I smile and thank God for what He has done in me to this point, but oh, the journey ahead is clear; more work is needed. I can clearly see that lukewarmness of heart and slothfulness in attitude will not get the high calling of God's desire operating in my life to its fullness. If we do not move forward when the grace of God is moving ahead then when will we set out?

We read in the book of Exodus when God moved by day or night, the people had to move also or they would be left behind to the dangers of the desert and all its perils. Ex.13:21 **By day the LORD went ahead of them in a pillar of cloud to guide them on their way and by night in a pillar of fire to give them light, so that they could travel by day or night.** It would have sounded foolish if some of the people would say, "Oh, just go ahead, I'll catch up later. I'll get into God's wilderness desert program when I get around to it." No, that attitude would not have worked. Why then do we take on that attitude today when the pillar of God is moving in our lives per se?

The desert was fraught with wild animals walking and stalking the fringes of the camp looking for easy prey. From a cackle of hyenas to a coalition of cheetahs ready to take down the weak traveling on their own in the wild of the desert was not wisdom nor a place to find oneself. Death through thirst and hunger would have been lurking as a constant possibility for anyone foolish enough to take on God's plan without God in it. These slow and rebellious people would be in constant danger of losing their way in God and life.

Why, then, do we think we can do the same today when God tells us it is time to move forward in His plan? Paul warns us that wolves would try to tear apart the body of Christ. Acts 20:29 **I know that after I leave, savage wolves will come in among you and will not spare the flock.** Peter warns us of the devil going about as a lion looking for the spiritually weak in heart. 1Pet. 5:8 **Be alert and of sober mind. Your enemy the devil prowls around like a roaring lion looking for someone to devour.**

These warnings and object lessons of wild animals the Apostles are using are meant to show us our adversary the devil is out to slow us down to a crawl, so we can be vulnerable and therefore pounced upon and destroyed mercilessly. Someone might say, "Well, I'm only an usher in the church, how could I slow down the plan of God in any one's life or my own life?" Maybe you were supposed to have been the music pastor and that is why the church assembly you attend is having a hard time breaking through when worship is going on.

The point is, that we are to flourish where we are planted and grow into what God is preparing for us and in us for today and the future. If you do not step up to the plate now, then when? Today is the day to act upon what God is doing because we only have today to do it. Psalm 118:24 **This is the day the Lord has made; we will rejoice and be glad in it.** To assume we can catch up to what God is doing in our life later on when we feel up to it is a form of arrogance that should not be part of our Christian nature.

We do not dictate to God when He can do a work within our soul. The Lord dictates to us when the time is right and now is the time for the next step of our walk in Him. Maybe God has been asking you to forgive a person who did you wrong or give back something you took that was never yours.

Maybe God is asking you to step out by faith and answer his knock on the door of your heart in order to take part in the next feast God has for your life. Rev. 3:20 **Here I am! I stand at the door and knock. If anyone hears my voice and opens the door, I will come in and eat with that person, and they with me.** If not now, then when will you enter into what God is doing for you and in you? If not now, when?

PART THREE:

QUESTIONS FOR UNDERSTANDING

1. *What did you learn in this section of the book?*
2. *What surprised you the most?*
3. *What subject(s) spoke to your heart?*
4. *Did the material that you read help you understand he subject(s) more or less?*
5. *What topics are important to you? Why?*
6. *How do these articles relate to you?*
7. *After reading this section of the book, what will you change in your life?*

PART FOUR:

TIMELESS PRINCIPLES

Stop Watering Dead Plants

RICHLY BLESSED

Proverbs 10:22 The blessing of the LORD makes one rich, and He adds no sorrow with it.

We are so richly blessed that we often do not see the blessings that are right in front of us. We have been given so much love and help from God, that our capacity to take it all in is beyond our comprehension. 2Pet. 1:3 **By his divine power, God has given us everything we need for living a godly life. We have received all of this by coming to know him, the one who called us to himself by means of his marvelous glory and excellence.**

Unfortunately, we don't always count our blessings, because they are immeasurable. Be that as it may, why are we no longer counting the blessings we do see in our lives? Have we become complacent with the generosity of God, and become blind to His goodness? I hope not, because the blessing of the Lord should make us rich in gratitude as well as in the provisions for living a blessed life.

We sometimes miss the greatness of God's

plan, because we are looking afar for answers that are close at hand. "The answer is in the house." This is one of my wife's expressions when looking for an answer to one of life's problems. Her faith is saying that God has already taken care of the problem. However, we just have to believe it by faith, and see how it manifests in God's timing. My wife sees this principle at work in the story of the widow in 2Kings 4:1-7.

There was a widow who had to pay off some big debts that the creditors had come to collect. She asks Elisha for help, and he says to her, "What do you have in the house?" 2Kings 4:2 **So Elisha said to her, "What shall I do for you? Tell me, what do you have in the house?" And she said, "Your maidservant has nothing in the house but a jar of oil."** Through faith, and a miracle of provision, the widow obeys Elisha and borrowed many large jars and fills the jars with oil. She did not stop pouring until the last jar was full. She was able to sell all the oil and pay off all she owed, plus have enough left to live on. Wow! The answer was in the house.

In another Scripture, Moses needs God's help and all he has is his shepherd's staff. Ex. 4:2 **Then the LORD asked him, "What is that in your hand?" "A shepherd's staff," Moses replied.** God used what Moses had within reach of Moses' hand to deliver Israel. The answer was in the house, so to speak. Moses did not have to go off on some quest and find a unique thing or weapon that would work against an Egyptian army. God was able to deliver a nation with what was available to Moses and that was his shepherd's staff. The blessing Moses needed was right there in his hand. With God, all things are possible. Matt. 19:26b **But with God all things are possible.** Gratefulness to God for what we do have is what God can use to richly bless us.

This is part of Earl Nightingale's article, *The Acres of Diamonds story "a true one" is told of an African farmer who heard tales about other farmers who had made millions by discovering diamond mines. These tales so excited the farmer that he could hardly wait to sell his farm and go prospecting for diamonds himself. He sold the farm and spent the rest of his life wandering the African continent searching unsuccessfully for the gleaming gems that brought such high prices on the markets of the world. Finally, worn out and in a fit of despondency, he threw himself into a river and drowned.*

Meanwhile, the man who had bought his farm happened to be crossing the small stream on the property one day, when suddenly there was a bright flash of blue and red light from the stream bottom. He bent down and picked up a stone. He had found one of the largest diamonds ever discovered. The farm the first farmer had sold so that he might find a diamond mine, turned out to be one of the most productive diamond mines on the entire African continent. The first farmer had owned, free and clear … acres of diamonds. But he had sold them for practically nothing, in order to look for them elsewhere.

What an amazing story of loss and gain. There are so many takeaways from this life lesson and significant teaching. How many people are walking through life looking for blessings that are right under their feet? In fact, they are walking in blessings galore but not able to see or appreciate them, because they have not been giving thanks to God for what they do have in life. 1 Thes. 5:18 **In every thing give thanks: for this is the will of God in Christ Jesus concerning you.**

I say it again, "We are richly blessed." The Lord has blessed us with so many blessings that if we were to start counting them today, we would still be counting until the day we died. Look at what God has done for us through Christ our Lord. Psalm 103:3 **He forgives all my sins and heals all my diseases. 4 He redeems me from death and crowns me with love and tender mercies.** These are just a few blessings we live in every day. Let us all proclaim this verse together and out loud! Prov. 10:22 **The blessing of the LORD makes one rich, and He adds no sorrow with it.** Amen and amen!

Norm Sawyer

THE WORD CAN HEAL OR STING

Proverbs 25:11 A word spoken at the right time is like gold apples on a silver tray.

Yiddish saying: The pen stings worse than an arrow.

What can we believe? In this overcharged world of information that runs at a pace no one is able to keep up with and comes in through many mediums can be overwhelming and disorienting. Our senses are inundated with information overload. God did warn us that there would be a time when information and knowledge would increase at gigabyte speeds. Dan. 12:4 **But you, Daniel, keep these words secret, and seal the book until the end times. Many will travel everywhere, and knowledge will grow.**

Yet, through all the information coming at us at a tsunami type strength, God's word is still distinguishable in our hearts because God's word is alive. Heb. 4:12 **For the word of God is alive and active. Sharper than any double-edged sword, it penetrates even to dividing soul and spirit, joints and marrow; it judges the**

thoughts and attitudes of the heart. The word of God is not dormant or lifeless. It breathes the love and intent of God's ultimate design and purpose for us all. The word is alive because Jesus is the word that came and lived among us. John 1:14 **The Word became flesh and took up residence among us. We observed His glory, the glory as the One and Only Son from the Father, full of grace and truth.**

God's word can be a balm to the soul or sting with noticeable force and conviction. This will cause repentance or outright anger and hatred toward God and His people. For the person who rejects God's word because of their personal views, lifestyle, or rebellion, the word of God can become a stinging experience within their conscience. The Lord's word does not always feel like comfort or healing if we are living contrary to its intent. There is a larger and substantial purpose that the word has than just a feel-good moment with God's love working in and through us. The word of God instructs, corrects, cleanses and trains us for a life of righteousness. 2Tim. 3:16 **All Scripture is God-breathed and is useful for teaching, rebuking, correcting and training in righteousness.**

The word of the Lord can be a healing balm through a hard time in life, or it can be an irksome presence reminding us of our shortcomings. How we respond to the work taking place in our hearts because of the living word working its purpose is up to our free will and choice within the relationship we have with the Lord. The personal relationship we have with the word of God is ours to receive with gladness or shun with an uncomfortable effort. Deut. 12:28 **Be careful to listen to all these words which I command you, so that it may be well with you and your sons after you forever, for you will be doing what is good and right in the sight of the LORD your God.**

What about our words towards each other? I saw a quote this week that reads, "Two things to remember in life: Take care of your thoughts when you're alone, and take care of your words when you're with others." Are our words life-lifting and inspiring or empty and life draining? Have we brought life to this hardened world with the holy language of God's love? The words that come out of our mouth can build up or tear down. We can encourage or bully our fellow man with healing or stinging words.

It seems like it is almost fashionable to belittle every honest effort made to improve the wellbeing of people's lives. However, as a human race, we can do better if we want to. We have to remember that God loves the whole world and our kind words are the balm and honey that will attract the world to God. John 3:16 **For God so loved the world, that he gave his only begotten Son, that whosoever believes in him should not perish, but have everlasting life.** Our words have the power of life and death. Let us be willing to have an over-abundant amount of life-giving words for each other and we will see the healing of the nations. Prov. 18:21 **The tongue has the power of life and death, and those who love it will eat its fruit.** Blessings to us all.

Norm Sawyer

AN ENCOURAGING WORD

Proverbs 11:25 The liberal soul shall be made fat: and he that waters shall be watered also himself.

There is nothing as heart healing as hearing the right word at the right time. In that moment of hearing a word of blessing, deliverance or assurance, we then know that we know God has heard our heart's cry and there is a peace that is beyond words of explanation that settles our hearts. Phil. 4:7 **And the peace of God, which passes all understanding, shall keep your hearts and minds through Christ Jesus.**

It is always nice to receive that word when we are in need, but just as nice to be the one giving it out and doing it from a heart of blessing. There is an amazing side factor of blessing that happens when someone gives out a blessing in word or action. The one who needed a word in season gets blessed and the one who gave it out also gets blessed, but most interesting is if anyone sees this blessing taking place they also get blessed.

Talk about paying-it-forward. This blessed result has a compounding effect. Blessing upon blessing goes out and will not come back empty. Isa. 55:11 **So shall my word be that goes forth out of my mouth: it shall not return unto me void, but it shall accomplish that which I please, and it shall prosper in the thing whereto I sent it.**

How hard is it to say something encouraging to anyone? It does not have to be spoken in eloquence or with great dialogue. It can be as simple as smiling and saying, "Good morning, I hope everything goes your way today." However, we get entangled in our busy lives and move forward without thought or seeing anything around us and live lives of mediocrity where we end up existing rather than living. Eccl. 11:4 **He that observes the wind shall not sow; and he that regards the clouds shall not reap.**

We end up doing nothing and getting the result of that non action. We are neither hot or cold as we become common in attitude and eventually empty of vision. Blessing should be on the tips of our tongues, ready to pounce like a mugger rather than giving grievous words of an empty value. Words of blessing will bring life to a bad situation and words inspired by God will bring people out of darkness into a great lifetime of light and blessing.

Prov. 4:20 **My son, attend to my words;**

---

incline thine ear unto my sayings. **22 For they are life unto those that find them, and health to all their flesh.** In many cases, we are the only bible that a lot of people in our lives ever get to read. Matt. 5:16 **Let your light so shine before men, that they may see your good works, and glorify your Father which is in heaven.**

What if Barnabas had never spoken out on behalf of Saul to the Apostles? Barnabas brought an encouraging word to the apostles as to the value and conversion of Saul. Barnabas also got the apostles to trust the reality of Saul's conversion. Acts 9:26 **And when Saul was come to Jerusalem, he assayed to join himself to the disciples: but they were all afraid of him, and believed not that he was a disciple. 27 But Barnabas took him, and brought him to the apostles, and declared unto them how he had seen the Lord in the way, and that he had spoken to him, and how he had preached boldly at Damascus in the name of Jesus.**

Those encouraging words changed history for the church and we now have an incredible amount of the New Testament written by Paul who now encourages us through the Holy Spirit.

What if Jesus, through His encouraging words, had not brought Peter out of his guilt for denying Christ three times? John 21:17 **He saith unto him the third time, Simon, son of Jonas, lovest thou me? Peter was grieved because he said unto him the third time, Lovest thou me? And he said unto him, Lord, you know all things; you know that I love thee. Jesus saith unto him, Feed my sheep.**

Jesus not only encouraged Peter but marked out his ministry for him and we know that Peter became a bold encourager in the Holy Spirit. Acts 4:14 **Now when they saw the boldness of Peter and John, and perceived that they were unlearned and ignorant men, they marvelled; and they took knowledge of them, that they had been with Jesus.** Notice had been taken that they had been with Jesus who had encouraged these unlearned men into powerful men of God in the Holy Spirit by His words.

Someone might say, "But that was Jesus, I am just me." Not so, we have Jesus living within our souls. The Spirit of God will guide us into all things that pertain to the wisdom and will of the Holy Spirit. Luke 12:12 **For the Holy Ghost shall teach you in the same hour what ye ought to say.** We just have to be willing vessels of the Holy Spirit and willing to be ready with a blessing from our hearts and on our tongues that will change a person's life or perspective forever. Start at home and just go bless someone. Blessings.

DOUBLE-TALK

Proverbs 3:28 Do not say to your neighbor, "Come back tomorrow and I'll give it to you"— when you already have it with you.

Bertrand Russell said, "Never try to discourage thinking, for you are sure to succeed."

We live in a time of perpetual confusion where duplicity and subterfuge is promoted as an acquired skill to survive in this world. We are at that place in our history where we call evil good and good evil. Isa. 5:20 **Woe unto them that call evil good, and good evil; that put darkness for light, and light for darkness; that put bitter for sweet, and sweet for bitter!**

We save whales and kill babies. Our governments allow the whims of the few to force unethical changes onto the moral majority. Our corrupt financial leaders protect and promote usurious lending and investment schemes they know are worthless. Big agriculture proclaims the safety and virtue of GMO products to the point of heirloom seed extinction. The big business of cancer saving drugs costing as much as a mortgage

is promoted as health care for us all.

All of these controversies are causing a numbness of the soul wherein Bertrand Russell might be right in that it is discouraging thinking among the masses. The apostle Paul explains this very event that is taking place in our times. 2 Tim. 3:2 **People will be lovers of themselves, lovers of money, boastful, proud, abusive, disobedient to their parents, ungrateful, unholy, 3 without love, unforgiving, slanderous, without self-control, brutal, not lovers of the good, 4 treacherous, rash, conceited, lovers of pleasure rather than lovers of God-- 5 having a form of godliness but denying its power. Have nothing to do with such people.**

I am very aware that there are honest and forthright people in each one of the professional fields mentioned above. Men and women who are truly called to these professions are trying with all their hearts to make a difference while working in a broken system that has become commonplace. When talking with and encouraging these courageous mavericks they often speak of the challenges they face because of all the double-talk and political wranglings that go on behind the scenes.

Duplicity and subterfuge are the spiritual giants they are battling on a daily basis. Eph. 6:12

For we wrestle not against flesh and blood, but against principalities, against powers, against the rulers of the darkness of this world, against spiritual wickedness in high places. May God give these honorable men and women the ability to overcome the perpetual lies raining down upon them and bring a blessed Godly reform needed in their workplaces.

What can we do as individuals to help change the status-quo of an insipid existence? How can I make sure I do not buy into this drone-like thinking and slothful humanism? One of the ways of beating this trend is to do what the word of God says to do and do it by faith. James 1:22 **Do not merely listen to the word, and so deceive yourselves. Do what it says.**

The Lord admonishes us to be vigilant in hearing what His Spirit is saying to us. There is a reward for those of us who overcome the temptation of being sluggish and shallow in our soul. Rev. 2:7 **He that hath an ear, let him hear what the Spirit saith unto the churches; To him that overcomes will I give to eat of the tree of life, which is in the midst of the paradise of God.**

By overcoming the temptation to live a compromising life we will be blessed with the privilege of eating the fruit from the tree of life.

Who is life? John 14:6 **Jesus answered, "I am the way and the truth and the life. No one comes to the Father except through me.** When a person receives life they will speak life and double-talk will be far removed from their hearts. We will taste and see that the Lord is good and will want more of His anointed goodness in our lives because we always want more of what tastes good, and God is good. Psalm 34:8 **Taste and see that the LORD is good; blessed is the one who takes refuge in him.**

Enough with all the double-talk and trying to manipulate our fellow man. Prov. 3:28 **Do not say to your neighbor, "Come back tomorrow and I'll give it to you"-- when you already have it with you.** Bring honesty to your workplace and see what the Lord can do with the power of one righteous person doing what is right in God's eyes. Stop being part of the rumor mill in your workplace and fellowship centers. Ex. 20:16 **You shall not give false testimony against your neighbor.**

Make a covenant with your own heart that you will be what God has called you to be. Make your communication plain and without double meanings, so you can be taken at your everyday honest word. Be the miracle that people need right now in the maze of all the multicultural confusion. The principles of God's word have never changed and we can count on the honesty of what God says to us to be true. Mal. 3:6a **For I am the Lord, I change not.** In Jesus name, may we all grasp and acquire the skill to talk as plainly as our Lord does and live in the peace and joy found in Christ. Amen.

WHAT CAN GOD DO?

Proverbs 8:35 For whoso finds me finds life, and shall obtain favor of the LORD.

What can God do in our situation? Luke 1:37 **For with God nothing shall be impossible.** A very short verse but speaks volumes. Gen. 18:14a **Is any thing too hard for the LORD?** Jer. 32:27 **Behold, I am the LORD, the God of all flesh: is there anything too hard for me?** When God asks a question that has the answer in the question, we have to submit to the truth of the Lord's promise that is in the verse. The part most of us struggle with is when we ask ourselves, "Would God actually do something for me?"

We rarely question God's ability to do anything. After all, we know God created the entire universe and all its intricacies. Deep down in our hearts, we all know nothing is impossible for God, but we wrestle with the question. Would God do something for me? Why would God even want to do something for me or in me? Does God want to actually help little old me? Am I even on God's radar? Oh! I can understand God wanting to do something for you because you are obviously one of His favorites, but for me, I am not sure.

The lie of the devil is hard at work and he has not changed his tactics in millenniums. He says with slithering whispers into your mind. "What can God do for you, after all, you know what you did yesterday." The devil brings up the lie that you are not good enough for the All-Mighty, or you will always be a loser because you were born wrong. On and on it goes.

The enemy of our soul is still doing the same old thing as in the garden of Eden. Gen. 3:4 **And the serpent said unto the woman, Ye shall not surely die.** What a lie that was and we are still falling for it. The reason we are attacked this way is that the devil knows full well that we do have absolute authority over the devil and his lies. We do have mighty weapons to defeat this onslaught of corruption from the father of lies. 2Cor. 10:4 **For the weapons of our warfare are not carnal, but mighty through God to the pulling down of strong holds;** 5 **Casting down imaginations, and every high thing that exalts itself against the knowledge of God, and bringing into captivity every thought to the obedience of Christ.**

If Satan actually had power over us Christians, why then does he have to deceive us into sinning?

Why does he not just go ahead and kill us? The reason is that he has no authority over us whatsoever. We are not under the authority of sin; we only wrestle the power of it. Rom. 8:1 **There is therefore now no condemnation to them which are in Christ Jesus, who walk not after the flesh, but after the Spirit.**

As my friend Jonathan likes to say, "What has the devil got to do with me? I am a king in the kingdom of God and Satan is only the prince of the air. Kings do not take orders from a prince. As a matter of fact, Kings give orders to the prince. Kings have authority over a prince as we have authority over the works of the prince of darkness." Luke 10:19 **Behold, I give unto you power to tread on serpents and scorpions, and over all the power of the enemy: and nothing shall by any means hurt you.**

What do we do with this kingdom authority? Matt. 10:7 **And as ye go, preach, saying, The kingdom of heaven is at hand. 8 Heal the sick, cleanse the lepers, raise the dead, cast out devils: freely ye have received, freely give.** We are kings and priests in the kingdom of our God. Rev.1:6 **And hath made us kings and priests unto God and his Father; to him be glory and dominion for ever and ever. Amen.** As kings and priests in the kingdom of God, we take our orders from a King - not a fallen prince. Jesus is the King of kings and Lord of lords. We do not need to look anywhere else for instruction in life.

Now, it comes back to those questions. "What can God do in and for me? Am I worth God's attention? Would God actually do a work on my behalf?" If we are under the blood of Christ, then we have a right standing with our God. With that right standing, we can seek first the kingdom and God's righteousness and that puts us in a position to receive all that the King of us kings has to offer.

If God can make the wolf be at peace with the lamb, then surely He can make our destructive wolves, per-se, come under the authority of our consecrated lives in Christ. Isa. 11:6 **In that day the wolf and the lamb will live together; the leopard will lie down with the baby goat. The calf and the yearling will be safe with the lion, and a little child will lead them all.** When we learn to live in the kingdom of our God and rule as kings with righteous motives, we will live a life of favor in the LORD. Luke 1:37 **For with God nothing shall be impossible.** Blessings upon us all.

KEEP THE WINDOWS OPEN

Proverbs 31:20 She stretches out her hand to the poor; yea, she reaches forth her hands to the needy.

Why does God admonish us to be generous and give freely from our heart to relieve the pain, grief and sometimes the needs of others? My friend Justin Long says by tithing and the giving of offerings God knows we are keeping the windows of heaven open above our lives for the blessing of God to fall on us and others. Mal. 3:10 **Bring the full tithe into the storehouse, that there may be food in my house. And thereby put me to the test, says the LORD of hosts, if I will not open the windows of heaven for you and pour down for you a blessing until there is no more need.**

It is interesting that God puts us in a position to be blessed. God helps us be generous so that generosity comes back to us. Eccl. 11:1 **Cast thy bread upon the waters: for thou shalt find it after many days.** God is trying to help us become like His Son Jesus who gave fully of

Himself to everyone who asked of him from an honest heart.

Generosity is a hard concept for many to understand in this selfish world we live in. This is the day and age of consumptive living and the glutenous slogans like "Take what you can get before it runs out" are all around us. Constant promotion of chasing wealth is surrounding us and it becomes harder to hear the soft sound of generosity and helpfulness toward each other. Jesus asks a good question in Mark 8:36 **For what does it profit a man to gain the whole world and forfeit his soul?**

What stuff out there in the world system is worth the price of your soul? How does a life of scheming and taking, keep the windows of heaven open over your life? It doesn't because hands that are closed cannot hold any more of anything, but hands that are open have room for more blessings to come your way to be enjoyed and passed on.

God tells us to take stock of our ways and methods and to make sure our ways are not a dead end. Hag. 1:5 **Now therefore thus saith the LORD of hosts; Consider your ways. 6 Ye have sown much, and bring in little; ye eat, but ye have not enough; ye drink, but ye are not filled with drink; ye clothe you, but**

there is none warm; and he that earns wages earns wages to put it into a bag with holes. If everything you are doing is resulting in a non-heavenly return then you have to stop and consider your ways.

Keep the windows of heaven open over your life and stay generous. Give of yourself to what is needed in the kingdom of God. If it is time, then give time. If it is a monetary need, then give it. If it is help then give of yourselves, but keep the windows of heaven open. Eccl. 11:2 **Give a portion to seven, and also to eight; for you do not know what evil shall be upon the earth.**

God seems to be saying to give to seven needs and ventures, give to eight and more because we do not know when trouble comes our way and we become the one in need. God forbid that this trouble should come but, if it does, we will have seven and eight giving to us during that time. We will be living under an open heaven because we had been living a generous life and now we are reaping what we had sown.

Oh, I know that it is not always that cut and dry because we do not see the beginning to the end. However, God says give and it shall be given to us. Luke 6:38 **Give, and it will be given to you. A good measure, pressed down, shaken**

together and running over, will be poured
into your lap. For with the measure you use,
it will be measured to you.

How did God make sure there would be an
open heaven over mankind? He gave generously
of Himself. John 3:16 **For God so loved the
world, that he gave his only begotten Son,
that whosoever believes in him should not
perish, but have everlasting life.** For God so
loved that He gave. There it is. God is a giver. We
are His children and we are to become givers like
our heavenly Father.

We are also to bring blessing in this greedy
world. The Apostle Paul reminds us of the words
of Jesus that it is more blessed to give than to
receive. Acts 20:35 **In everything I did, I showed
you that by this kind of hard work we must
help the weak, remembering the words the
Lord Jesus himself said: 'It is more blessed
to give than to receive.**

This is often heard with a bit of skepticism
in our Western thinking. However, Paul, who
evangelized most of the known world in his
day, had seen the power of giving and he lived
under an open heaven during his whole ministry.
Giving became his way of life and because of
Paul's generosity, we are still enjoying the fruit
of his ministry today. Yes, Lord, help us remain

generous while we are on this earth and keep the windows of heaven open above us. Amen!

THE FOOL AND HIS FOLLY

Proverbs 26:4 Don't answer a fool according to his foolishness or you'll be like him yourself.

Yiddish saying: "If he were twice as smart, he'd be an idiot!"

The Apostle Paul warned us about arguing over words, or as some call it, "Alternative facts." Truth is truth. Whether someone hears the truth or not, it is not up to us to enforce it, but rather to live by it. Jesus said in the Gospel of John: "The Holy Spirit would do all the convicting, convincing, and reproving." John 16:8 **And when he is come, he will reprove the world of sin, and of righteousness, and of judgment.**

Christians are to influence the world with the love we have for one another. We are to be ready to explain and demonstrate why we love the Lord and the reasons for the joy and peace that leads us toward following Christ, regardless of circumstances. 2Tim. 2:14 **Keep reminding God's people of these things. Warn them before God against quarreling about words; it is of no value, and only ruins those who** listen.16 **But shun profane and vain babblings: for they will increase unto more ungodliness.**

The reason we are instructed to not argue, fight, and bully concerning the word of God is simple; arguing with a fool will go nowhere and amount to nothing. Prov. 26:4 **Don't answer a fool according to his foolishness or you'll be like him yourself.** If a person has chosen to speak out his folly by declaring there is no God, then we are dealing with a soul issue that only God Himself can heal.

Psalm 14:1 **The fool says in his heart, "There is no God." They are corrupt, they do abominable deeds; there is none who does good.** This kind of stubbornness is deeply influenced by the enemy of our soul and only the love of God can break through such hardness of heart. The Holy Spirit can shed light on the hidden darkness of any soul.

The world is awash in foolishness and half-truths that have become mainstream. In some circles foolishness has become the normal direction being chosen by governments, school boards, and numerous companies who have through legislation maneuvered their ways into our lives.

Big medicine, agriculture, banking, and industry have lobbied their way into positions of influence and have moved into our everyday normal existence. Day by day we become deeply connected to these systems and must keep our spiritual ear tuned to what the Holy Spirit is saying so that we do not become wholeheartedly dependent on them for the nourishment of our souls.

We often cringe at the foolish choices being made by our leaders and authorities and realize why God instructs us to pray for them. They do not have the wisdom of God; therefore, are found in need of divine help. 1Tim. 2:1 **First of all, then, I urge that supplications, prayers, intercessions, and thanksgivings be made for all people,** 2 **for kings and all who are in high positions, that we may lead a peaceful and quiet life, godly and dignified in every way.** God asks us to pray for our leaders so that we may live peaceful lives. It does not guarantee there will be peace on earth, but rather we would remain in peace regardless of what foolishness is manifesting. Pray for them so we may be at peace.

Peace is not the absence of war. The world's example of peace is living without war and is the only peace the world can offer. However, real peace can be had within our beings in any place and time if we are fully in Christ. Matt. 5:9 **Blessed**

are the peacemakers: for they shall be called the children of God. The world system, often through its own methods, brings great chaos and harm to multitudes of people. Then when there is mayhem, they turn around and blame God for the terrible consequences inflicted on humanity. Now that is foolishness on a grand scale.

Saints, the fool and his folly is all around us because the wisdom of God is not accepted as truth. People claim to have their own truth and will argue their view to the point of ridiculousness. Prov. 14:12 **There is a way that appears to be right, but in the end it leads to death.**

In Christ, we have a great and wonderful God whose love we have responded to. Yes, there will be times when we will be foolish and do foolish things, but God will guide us into all truth if we let Him. The Kingdom of God is not just all about talk. It is a Kingdom of power and blessing that can remove foolishness from our hearts. 1Cor. 4:20 **For the Kingdom of God is not just a lot of talk; it is living by God's power.** May we all become wise in the name of the Lord. Amen!

THE DISCIPLINED

Proverbs 13:24 Those who spare the rod of discipline hate their children. Those who love their children care enough to discipline them.

Rodney King: "I just want to say, can't we all get along?"

It will be very difficult for all to get along because it takes discipline to do so. I was reading in the Gospel of Luke where the disciples were arguing as to who was greater. Luke 9:46 **An argument started among the disciples as to which of them would be the greatest.** Gal. 5:26 **Let us not be desirous of vain glory, provoking one another, envying one another.** The thought struck me that even in the company of Jesus it still took discipline to control their volatile emotions and it took willpower to overcome the temptations of power and control.

We are, after all, created in the image of God and were given dominion on the earth. So the desire to take control and create something from our hearts comes honestly. The problem, of course, came with the fall of man and man's desire was corrupted to the point of even wanting God under our feet. Isa. 14:12 **How art thou fallen from heaven, O Lucifer, son of the morning! how art thou cut down to the ground, which didst weaken the nations! 13 For thou hast said in thine heart, I will ascend into heaven, I will exalt my throne above the stars of God: I will sit also upon the mount of the congregation, in the sides of the north: 14 I will ascend above the heights of the clouds; I will be like the most High.**

Because of our fallen nature that was corrupted by this narcissistic sinful angel Lucifer, we now need to be disciplined by God in order to walk in the power of the Holy Spirit. The good news is that we have been given grace to walk out our Christian lives as we learn to be disciples in Christ. It is as if we were granted the privilege and blessing to learn how to play the violin in public with none of the harsh criticisms and vitriolic shouts to shut up!

We were saved and we are being saved and we will be saved because of this grace that we are covered in. The discipline or rod of correction over our lives is not irksome or harsh. It is the blessing of the Lord that corrects us. Prov. 3:12 **For the LORD disciplines the one He loves, just as a father, the son he delights in.** Some of us might have a negative connotation as to the meaning of the word discipline. Many think of childhood beatings that left unresolved anger and lifelong scars. That is not what God does.

The reader's digest version for the word discipline is: In its natural sense, discipline is systematic instruction intended to train a person, sometimes literally called a disciple, in a craft, trade or other activity, or to follow a particular code of conduct. We are all being disciplined to be like Jesus and Jesus did everything out of love.

His guidance in our lives will also be motivated the same way; out of love. Why would God use love to discipline us? 1John 4:18 **There is no fear in love; but perfect love casts out fear: because fear hath torment. He that fears is not made perfect in love.** This is why we can trust the discipline of the Lord because it will eventually produce love. Will the discipline always feel good? No! However, the fruit and results will be glorious and eternal.

I have shared this before but it is worth repeating. I was angry at myself one day because I had sinned. I heard the Spirit of God ask me, "Are you angry because you vexed the Holy Spirit or are you angry because you broke your personal righteousness record?" It was clear that I did not care about vexing the Holy Spirit because the question would not have been asked. It looked like I was in for some correction with the rod of God's love. Was I embarrassed, ashamed and feeling a bit uncertain? Yup! All three feelings were screaming in my head, but God loved me through it by reaching my heart. I repented and peace came just as our loving Father said it would. Phil. 4:7 **And the peace of God, which passes all understanding, shall keep your hearts and minds through Christ Jesus.**

Don't be afraid of the correction and discipline that comes from our Lord. It is life to our very being and it will get us through all the battles that come our way. God is good! Blessings.

GIVING AWAY AN INHERITANCE

Proverbs 14:18 The simple inherit folly: but the prudent are crowned with knowledge.

Confucius said, "If your plan is for one year, plant rice. If your plan is for ten years, plant trees. If your plan is for one hundred years, educate children."

A hundred year plan in this "I want it now" generation might be hard to plan for. It is not necessarily this generation's fault. They are bombarded with "you can have it now with no money down" advertisements on a twenty-four-seven timeline and live-streaming on all of their communication devices.

This next generation needs to be able to make it through their lives and get through it with the right choices. By saying this I might sound like an old guy with the normal anxiousness about the up and coming generation, but I am trying to help educate the next generation toward righteousness. I am attempting to leave them an inheritance of Godly value.

Keeping our minds steadfast and contemporary

at the same time can be difficult because of the fast acceleration of change going on all around us. However, the principles of God's word do not change. The word of God can be counted on to meet the needs of any generation, right now and going forward into the long and distant future. Heb. 13:8 **Jesus Christ is the same yesterday and today and forever.**

As I get older I have reflected on what it was that gave me hope for the future I am now living in. Rightly so I did not have the massive amounts of choices and diversions available to young people today, but I still had to allow God entry into my soul. What I did have was the word of God helping me make prudent choices as I progressed through life. Did I get everything right? Absolutely not! There were some very big mistakes made along the way, but God's grace was there to help me through it all. I did learn a few things that are important to God and now to myself.

Leaving an inheritance of blessing to the next generation can be difficult if they do not want what we have. If I cannot get the next generation interested in a one year plan of victorious righteous living, then how can I ever get a ten or one hundred year plan going? If we are trying to convey the importance of righteous choices, then we had better have some fruit in our own lives that show what we are saying is true and worth having. Talk is cheap, but victory is powerful. Prov. 8:21 **That I may cause those that love me to inherit substance; and I will fill their treasures.**

It is said that children suffer the consequences of their parents' actions. If this is true in a family setting, how much more in a state, province or national setting? We have got to offer the next generation something of substance and worth that builds character of heart, rather than just more of the everyday fluff. We must show them the value of seeking God first in their lives. Matt. 6:20 **But store up for yourselves treasures in heaven, where moth and rust do not destroy, and where thieves do not break in and steal.**

Is who you have become in Christ worth sharing with the next generation? Do you have real joy in the Lord or is what you have an irksome existence? Are we translating the love of God and the fact that God is worth our whole world? Unless the next generation clearly sees the fullness of God working in our lives, why then would they want what we stand for? We need to complete each other and not compete with each other.

We have a great and wonderful inheritance in

Christ that was given to us all by grace. Eph. 3:7 **I became a servant of this gospel by the gift of God's grace given me through the working of his power.** Surely we can hand this gift over to the next generation with the same grace. If we live our lives in an honest covenant with the Lord our Savior, then the fruit of that relationship will be coveted by others who are looking for something real. Leave a real inheritance for the next generation that they can count on to give them life. Blessings.

LIFE MOVES ON

Proverbs 15:24 The path of life leads upward for the prudent to keep them from going down to the realm of the dead.

While crawling along the four-lane two-way street, I leaned back in my seat with one hand on the steering wheel as the traffic crept along. The congestion on both sides of the median was snarled. I was late for an appointment and there were no detours in sight. Next to me in the left lane, there was a funeral cortège. I could see the coffin through the tinted long side window of the black polished hearse as it moved at the same pace I was creeping along. I looked over and said, "Ya, for you, this traffic no longer matters, but for me and everyone in this gridlock, life goes on."

The fact is - like the person being carried away in the hearse, the day that I leave this earth, life will go on without me. A few people in my family and some friends will feel my absence for a while, but eventually, life will go on. James 4:14 **Yet you do not know what tomorrow will bring. What**

is your life? For you are a mist that appears for a little time and then vanishes. We all have an appointed time to fulfill what God has sown in our souls. After we leave this earthbound existence, God's worldwide eternal project continues without us. Hopefully, we were able to do what the Lord had instructed our hearts to do while we lived on His green earth.

Life moves on, with or without us, but while we are here, we use the wisdom God gives us to sow His love into this world while looking upward and forward toward our eternity. Prov. 15:24 **The path of life leads upward for the prudent to keep them from going down to the realm of the dead.** Hopefully, we do not live our lives in the realms of the dead but walk in a relationship with God. We have all been created on purpose, with a purpose, and for a purpose by our Heavenly Father. Our Lord has an eternal plan He sees us fulfilling. It is up to us to move forward by faith and enter the fullness of His plan through Christ.

Can God bring His eternal intentions to fruition without us, and can we be replaced? Absolutely! God is blessing our lives by allowing us to work with Him. How precious is that? Elijah believed he was alone in serving God and thought the Lord might be in trouble without his help. However, God pointed out that there were seven thousand others who were ministering with God in Israel at the time and God's program was moving forward. 1Kings 19:18 **Yet I reserve seven thousand in Israel—all whose knees have not bowed down to Baal and whose mouths have not kissed him.**

Fulfilling our life's purpose the best way we can, gives us life now and an expectation toward our eternity. However, we need to merge with what God is doing and stop heading off in other directions trying to manipulate what God is doing to coincide with our ambitions. We tend to want to control and know everything about our destiny in Christ. We seem to get in the way of what God is doing with our lives, loved ones, and time schedules. We need God's thoughts to move forward at the same pace God is moving. Isa. 55:8 **For my thoughts are not your thoughts, neither are your ways my ways, declares the LORD.** Getting out of God's way, and working within His master plan will bring results.

Some people want to know their future. Not me, no way! I want God to know my future and be in charge of it because I trust Him to fulfil it. King Hezekiah was dying and he asked God for more time to live. 2Kings 20:6a **I will add fifteen years to your life.** Hezekiah is granted fifteen more years of life. Think about it. Was it real life he got, or some extra time of existence? Yuk, could you imagine knowing the exact amount of time or the approximate date left till you die? In most cases, people would become paralyzed in thought by overanalyzing everything while knowing the upcoming death date was just off in the future. That little worm would eat away at their consciousness with a tick-tock tick-tock awareness that the fifteen years were coming to an end. I think this would make it hard to allow the joys of living in the moment to ever become restful in one's heart. The sad thing is, during this extra time Hezekiah drew breath, he fathered a son who would become the evilest king in Israel's history.

Yes, Lord, we all want a long and healthy life and thank God that we can pray for that blessing. But as for me Lord, let my concentration be on living in the spirit of God and not on the eventual date of my death. I'm speaking from the position of one who years ago did die for a moment while having a stroke. I know I am on borrowed time and I am making the best of living day by day and not keeping an eye on my expiration date. No Saints, today is the day the Lord has made and we are to rejoice in it. As life moves on, let us give our lives to the Lord and let Him direct our steps because He has the number of our days in His hands, and is well able to choose the best for us. May we all fulfill what the Lord created us to do and be in Him. Amen!

PART FOUR:

QUESTIONS FOR UNDERSTANDING

1. *What did you learn in this section of the book?*
2. *What surprised you the most?*
3. *What subject(s) spoke to your heart?*
4. *Did the material that you read help you understand the subject(s) more or less?*
5. *What topics are important to you? Why?*
6. *How do these articles relate to you?*
7. *After reading this section of the book, what will you change in your life?*

PART FIVE:

REST IN YOUR SALVATION

Stop Watering Dead Plants

When we sit down and enjoy the company of a good friend over an espresso at an outdoor cafe, we rest easily. The Lord wants us to be at rest in our salvation that Christ provided for us, and sit down with our God and love His company. Heb. 4:19 For all who have entered into God's rest have rested from their labors, just as God did after creating the world.

IMITATE ME

Proverbs 8:33 Listen to my instruction and be wise; do not disregard it.

The Apostle Paul said, "Imitate me." 1Cor. 4:16 **I urge you, then, be imitators of me.** The early Christians did not have the full New Testament at the ready to find out the way to deal with different situations in life. Some of the assemblies and gatherings of like-minded Christians had a letter or two from the Apostle Paul. Other Apostles like Peter, James, and John had written God-inspired epistles by the anointing of the Holy Spirit. However, no one had the complete collection of writings as we have today.

What did Paul have in his heart to be able to say with confidence- "Imitate me" 1Cor. 11:1 **You are to imitate me, just as I imitate Christ.** That was the key. Paul was saying, just as I imitate Christ, imitate what you see me being and doing as a result of Christ living through me. Paul said that once Christ becomes the Lord of our life, we will be read and scrutinized by the world. 2Cor. 3:2 **Ye are our epistle written in our hearts,**

known and read of all men: 3 you show that you are Christ's letter, delivered by us, not written with ink but with the Spirit of the living God—not on tablets of stone but on tablets of human hearts.

Would you have the confidence in Christ to boldly say to someone, "Imitate me, because I imitate Christ." Wow! What a responsibility we have as living epistles and letters of God that express His love for all of mankind. What are the people reading in us when they are looking for answers to life? Do as I say and not as I do, does not work here.

Imitate me as I walk in Christ, is imitating what I say and do. Of course, we are fallible people. When we fall, do those who are reading us see us repent, get up, and go forward in Christ? Do they see us making up excuses, shifting the blame, and shrinking back from our accountability to God and each other? I hope they see Christ at work within us doing what the Lord has instructed us to do in His name.

Our heart and confidence in the Lord should be a declaration that gently says, "Trust in the Lord, and listen to His instructions as you see me following Him with all my heart." Prov. 8:33 **Listen to my instruction and be wise; do not disregard it.** We are not talking about comparing ourselves with others, but rather sharpening and encouraging each other in the admonition of the love and power of God in order to be epistles that can be read clearly, as we point to Christ. Prov. 27:17 **Iron sharpens iron; so a man sharpens the countenance of his friend.**

As I get older, I have found it important to teach, direct, and give away everything I know about my Lord Jesus to the next generation. I am not trying to create clones of myself, but rather help develop the calling and gifting that is in every individual God has created. Jer. 29:11 **"For I know the plans I have for you"—this is the LORD's declaration—"plans for your well-being, not for disaster, to give you a future and a hope.**

The thoughts and intent of God's heart toward everyone is that none of us should perish, or be eternally lost. 2Pet. 3:9 **The Lord does not delay his promise, as some understand delay, but is patient with you, not wanting any to perish but all to come to repentance.** God has made a way for all mankind to come to Him through Christ. We who walk in Christ are His hand extended and read of men. May we remember this awesome responsibility the next time we open the pages of our heart to allow a lost and hurting world to read of God's grace that is available to them. What will be read from your living epistle? Blessings to you in Jesus name!

I AM CONTAGIOUS

Proverbs 7:4 Say to wisdom, "You are my sister," and call insight your intimate friend.

Acts 19:11 **God gave Paul the power to perform unusual miracles.** 12 **When handkerchiefs or aprons that had merely touched his skin were placed on sick people, they were healed of their diseases, and evil spirits were expelled.** Talk about being contagiously powerful in God! What a way to beat any and all diseases. I want to infect people with God's presence, love, healing, and wisdom to do beyond all our expectations. I want to be contagious with the anointing of the Lord and influence the people I meet with God's richness.

People either want to be around you or find a place far away from you. It really depends on what you are spreading while you are present. When you are in the room, are people growing in their hearts or are they groaning in their spirit because you are bringing them down in their faith? Prov. 27:17 **Iron sharpens iron, and one person sharpens another.** Hopefully, you are the reason others are becoming sharp in the Lord!

The effect that Solomon had on the surrounding nations was contagious. His wisdom was legendary and those who had the opportunity to stand in his presence and hear his wisdom were changed forever. The Queen of Sheba expressed it beautifully. 1Kings 10:6 **She said to the king, "The report I heard in my own country about your achievements and your wisdom is true. 7 But I did not believe these things until I came and saw with my own eyes. Indeed, not even half was told me; in wisdom and wealth you have far exceeded the report I heard.**

The most interesting comment concerning her observations was the fact that she noticed those who worked and served in Solomon's presence lived in an environment of wisdom and that made the people happy and wise. 1Kings 10:8 **How happy your people must be! How happy your officials, who continually stand before you and hear your wisdom!** Solomon's wisdom was contagious because it was the wisdom of God at work. Imagine being that infectious. To be able to influence people's hearts toward God.

That is the kind of righteous influence I want to have in my walk with the Lord. I want to contagiously affect the people I meet, by leading them into the presence of God. Wouldn't it be wonderful to have God's wisdom at work within our hearts and minds in the fulness of what the Queen of Sheba saw working within the whole royal court? We need to become that contagious in the Lord no matter the situation we are in or where we walk. Eph. 6:15 **And with your feet fitted with the readiness that comes from the gospel of peace.**

When you bring the Lord's blessings wherever you go, you are influencing the people to want to know God. As was with the Apostle Paul, who brought healing by the handkerchiefs or aprons that had merely touched his skin, we too can become that contagious in the Lord. Saints, the thing is, we have to want it! Prov. 7:4 **Say to wisdom, "You are my sister," and call insight your intimate friend.**

Heavenly Father, in Jesus name, help us become more infectious than any disease that is on earth at this time. Help us spread the love of God, rather than the wrath the enemy has been sowing throughout this world. Let us bring healing and joy wherever we go and may we imitate what was done by the apostles who changed the world with your word and grace. Acts 5:15 **As a result, they would carry the sick out into the streets and lay them on cots and mats so that when**

Peter came by, at least his shadow might fall on some of them. 16 In addition, a multitude came together from the towns surrounding Jerusalem, bringing the sick and those who were tormented by unclean spirits, and they were all healed. Amen!

NO CALL-WAITING

Proverbs 8:34 Blessed is the man that hears me, watching daily at my gates, waiting at the posts of my doors.

I have been waiting for years and still, this prayer has not been fulfilled to my expectation. Waiting on the Lord is all I ever do and still, I don't see my prayers answered. Maybe my request is not worth His attention. Maybe He is too busy with other important problems. I seem to be on constant hold and listening to a busy signal.

These are some of the biggest lies the devil will tell you as you wait on God, implying that you are not worth the Lord's time. Interesting, why is the devil so concerned about you getting through to God and being fulfilled? The devil is a liar from the beginning and the father of lies. He knows that your waiting on God is producing the patience of a Godly satisfaction. James 1:3 **Knowing this, that the trying of your faith works patience.**

One great thing about the Lord Jesus, He will never put you on call-waiting while many of His other sons and daughters are asking for His attention. He will never be too busy to hear your heart in prayer. You will always have His full attention. Isa. 65:24 **And it shall come to pass, that before they call, I will answer; and while they are yet speaking, I will hear.**

It might seem long to you, but you were heard by Him from the first thought you had about speaking with your God. Dan. 10:12 **Then said he unto me, Fear not, Daniel: for from the first day that thou didst set thine heart to understand, and to chasten thyself before thy God, thy words were heard, and I am come for thy words**.

Waiting on the Lord is not irksome when you know that He is waiting for you to come and let Him know everything that is going on in your mind and heart. Heb. 14:6 **Let us therefore come boldly unto the throne of grace, that we may obtain mercy, and find grace to help in time of need.** You will not shock the Lord with anything you say to Him because He knows you better than you know yourself.

He knows the "why" you are the way you are, and He has the answer to the difficulty you find yourself to be in. Jer. 33:3 **Call unto me, and I will answer thee, and shew thee great and mighty things, which thou knows not.**

The best part of this is that God will also fix the reason you keep falling into that difficulty, if you let Him.

Waiting is a state of being. Waiting on God is not a hanging around doing nothing verb. It is an action of faith in whom I am waiting on. I am at peace while waiting, because I know that the Lord heard me when I asked Him for help. 1John 5:14 **And this is the confidence that we have in him, that, if we ask any thing according to his will, he hears us:** 15 **And if we know that he hear us, whatsoever we ask, we know that we have the petitions that we desired of him.**

What if it was not His will as to what we are waiting and asking for. No matter, keep bringing your requests to the Lord so that you can find out how to ask within His will. Your teenagers did it with you as you were parenting them when they were growing up and waiting for their sixteenth birthday.

Dad, may I have the car tonight?

No, you do not have a driver's licence yet.

If I get a licence will I be able to drive the car?

That depends on your maturity at that time. I know, that sounded so fatherly but you get my meaning.

There are similarities here, as to when your maturity and ability to receive the answered prayer of the Lord is, in fact, a life building benefit. It is true that God gives us good things and other blessings for our lives. James 1:17 **Every good gift and every perfect gift is from above, and comes down from the Father of lights, with whom is no variableness, neither shadow of turning.** That is the beauty of waiting on the Lord because you are being prepared for the responsibility of that answered prayer.

There is that old adage that says, "Be careful what you wish for, because you just might get it." This truth has undone many a good person because they got so much, so fast, and suffered because they were not ready for the responsibility of what came with what they had wished for.

You might ask me if I've got this down in my life? No, not yet, but I am understanding it better and bringing everything to the Lord in prayer while waiting on Him. I can see its benefits to my growth in the Lord for His purpose and my well-being.

I find myself asking a lot of questions about this waiting for God's answers, but there seems to be a verse for that also. James 1:5 **If any of you lack wisdom, let him ask of God, that gives to all men liberally, and upbraids not; and it shall be given him.** 6a **But let him ask**

in faith, nothing wavering. Help us Lord be at peace while we wait on your direction and supply for our lives. In Jesus name. Amen.

HOMECOMING

Proverbs 31:25 Strength and honour are her clothing; and she shall rejoice in time to come.

Someone said, "Home is a place you grow up wanting to leave, and grow old wanting to get back to."

Throughout the year we look forward to homecomings. A lot of people are waiting for someone to come home and celebrate Thanksgiving, Christmas, New Year's and birthdays. There is hope and anticipation of renewed affection toward all the ones we love and miss. As a father, I am looking forward to seeing my sons who live far away and out of Province. As we look over the menus of the banquets and feasts that will be served, we try to have the favorite treats and delights for the ones who will be coming home for the reason of celebration.

As I think about these things I see our heavenly Father doing the same thing for those of us who have asked Christ into our hearts as Savior. Jesus is anticipating our homecoming and is preparing a place for us. John 14:2 **In my Father's house** are many mansions: if it were not so, I would have told you. I go to prepare a place for you. The Lord desires to be with us. John 14:3 **And if I go and prepare a place for you, I will come again, and receive you unto myself; that where I am, there ye may be also.**

As the old hymn says, *"Oh what a day that will be when my Jesus I shall see, and I look upon his face, the one who saved me by his grace. When he takes me by the hand and leads me through the promised land, what a day, glorious day that will be."* What a homecoming that will be when we all come home and live the eternal fulfilled life that Christ has for each one of us. There will be delightful treats for us. Rev. 2:7 **He that hath an ear, let him hear what the Spirit saith unto the churches; To him that overcomes will I give to eat of the tree of life, which is in the midst of the paradise of God.**

We will be given gifts, blessings and responsibilities. Luke 19:17 **And he said unto him, Well, thou good servant: because thou hast been faithful in a very little, have thou authority over ten cities.** We will be commissioned to expand and be part of the Kingdom of God throughout eternity, enjoying the very presence of God and each other. Rev. 21:23 **And the city had no need of the sun, neither of the moon, to shine in it: for the**

glory of God did lighten it, and the Lamb is the light thereof. 24 And the nations of them which are saved shall walk in the light of it: and the kings of the earth do bring their glory and honour into it.

What a homecoming that will be for all who have confessed Jesus Christ as Lord. Therefore, because we are in Christ and have this hope in our hearts, we can live in anticipation of being a blessing in life and living a blessed life that honors our God. Like Abraham, by faith, we look for the city, place, or location that God has for us in His Kingdom. Heb. 11:10 **For he looked for a city which hath foundations, whose builder and maker is God.** We do this so that we may be transformed into the image of Jesus Christ our Lord and fulfill God's purpose in our lives. Rom. 12:2 **And be not conformed to this world: but be ye transformed by the renewing of your mind, that ye may prove what is that good, and acceptable, and perfect, will of God.**

We live our lives in anticipation of this glorious homecoming that when it comes to pass it will draw pure love and exuberance from our hearts and souls. The magnificence of it all will take an eternity to appreciate and understand the wonders of the Lord's very being and what He did for each one of us He saved.

The presence of the Lord so affected Paul that he had no idea whether he was in or out of his body. It was overwhelming to him. 2Cor. 12:2 **I know a man in Christ who was caught up into the third heaven 14 years ago. Whether he was in the body or out of the body, I don't know, God knows. 4 Was caught up into paradise. He heard inexpressible words, which a man is not allowed to speak.**

Wow! Beyond explanation, and we are headed there. What a day that will be when my Jesus I shall see. I can say it with joy and happiness of heart. I am looking forward to seeing each one of you there one day. I will be looking for you. Hlovate said, "As truth be told, homecoming never gets old." Blessings.

A YEAR IN REVIEW

Proverbs 15:30 The light of the eyes rejoices the heart: and a good report makes the bones fat.

It is always a pitiful scene when the news cameras are focused on family members picking through the destruction of their homes after a tornado has devastated a town or community. These victims wander around with the odd item of personal value clutched to their sides with looks of bewilderment. Inevitably, the news reporters with a limited vocabulary asks one of these traumatised people, "How do you feel?"

I think this to be a dumb question, but the answer is almost always, "Well, everyone in the family is alive and that's what's important. All this, (as they point to the destruction), is just stuff that can be replaced." Then, the other question the news reporter learned in reporter-school asks, "What are you going to do now?" With a brave face, the answer is often, "We're going to rebuild."

Like most of you, I often ask, why rebuild in a place called Tornado Alley? Are they not setting themselves up for this to happen all over again?

Some of these people admit to the fact that this devastation has happened to them before. Oh well, we do not know the hearts and reasons these hearty people choose to rebuild and start over, but that is their free choice. Eccl. 5:19 **Every man also to whom God hath given riches and wealth, and hath given him power to eat thereof, and to take his portion, and to rejoice in his labour; this is the gift of God**.

As we muse and walk through the events of everyone's turbulent year, it is my hope that we are not wandering in bewildered at the destruction or loss of our spiritual effect on our family, friends, and workmates. Hopefully, we have good reports and testimonies of how God is faithful toward us all year long. I hope we have garnered a heart of gratitude toward those who love us and toward God who has saved us. Eph. 5:20 **Giving thanks always for all things unto God and the Father in the name of our Lord Jesus Christ.**

If we have experienced spiritual loss through repeated sin because we rebuilt in the same place as in our personal Tornado Alley, then it might be time to move. If some of us are finding it difficult to overcome tempting fruit that causes us to fall repeatedly, then it might be time to get out of that orchard and focus on redemption rather than self-righteousness, rebuilding on the same spot called mayhem. Job 11:14 **If iniquity be in thine hand, put it far away, and let not wickedness dwell in thy tabernacles.**

What have we discovered about ourselves throughout this last year? Were we kind, generous, and patient with one another? Did we go out of our way to bless those who bother us? Did we overcome in times of temptation? What progress in Christ have we made this past year that brings out a heartfelt assurance that we are walking the Lord's path of righteousness?

Minister Phil Drysdale says, "Spiritual maturity is not a process of you working on your sin - it's a process of you discovering your righteousness!" 2Cor. 5:21 **For he hath made Him to be sin for us, who knew no sin; that we might be made the righteousness of God in Him.** Christ, our Lord, has already paid for our sin, now let us grow in His grace-filled righteousness. Let us, through His grace and faith in His righteousness, appropriate the ability given to us to overcome sin. Keep our eyes on the cure for our lives and not the sickness that drags us down.

I can look back this year and see events that blessed me. For example, my sons and best friends came home to celebrate my birthday. My sons both landed wonderful jobs with very good companies. My darling wife of forty-one years still loves me and encourages me. I could go on and record so many great events that took place in my life this year, but did I grow in the righteousness of the Lord and His finished work of the cross? Mark 8:36 **For what shall it profit a man, if he shall gain the whole world, and lose his own soul?**

I can say there are areas I did grow in this year and there are areas I still need great leaps and strides of maturity in order to walk in the peace of righteousness that has been given to me through Christ. Rom. 5:17 **For if by one man's offence death reigned by one; much more they which receive abundance of grace and of the gift of righteousness shall reign in life by one, Jesus Christ. 18 Therefore as by the offence of one judgment came upon all men to condemnation; even so by the righteousness of one the free gift came upon all men unto justification of life.**

What a year of contrasts it has been for a lot of us who love the Lord and long for His coming. We have all had some great victories and some hurtful falls. What then shall we do? Shout, praise the Lord for all our victories, and dust ourselves off from the falls with a prayer on our lips and faith in our hearts declaring that we shall have better times ahead. Phil. 3:13 **Brethren, I count** not myself to have apprehended: but this one thing I do, forgetting those things which are behind, and reaching forth unto those things which are before, 14 **I press toward the mark for the prize of the high calling of God in Christ Jesus.** Amen!

ALL THAT MAY BE DESIRED

Proverbs 8:11 For wisdom is better than rubies; and all the things that may be desired are not to be compared to it.

We all have an over-imaginative thought process when it comes to the wants that may be within our hearts and minds. We can sure come up with a wish-list if we were to start writing down all that may be desired. Yet, the Proverb tells us to desire wisdom rather than rubies, silver, and gold. Prov. 8:10 **Receive my instruction, and not silver; and knowledge rather than choice gold.**

Surely if I had a lot of silver and gold, I could get all that I desire. How many people say, "If I could just have that new thing, then I would be happy." Would we be happy if we got absolutely everything we wanted without delay? I'm not sure, because I have never experienced that luxury.

I was walking through an auto junkyard with a friend who was looking for an '86 Pontiac Parisienne tail light. As I looked over all the rust and bent car frames, I became aware that at one time a lot of these cars had been wanted and coveted with motives spurred on by avarice. These broken and rusted shells that had once been dreams and goals of individuals had now been long forgotten.

Some of these cars had been desired to the point of theft, crooked dealings and over-extended credit; just to own that car that would bring happiness. Now, these idols of imagination were being picked over and rusting away through oxidation. Where was the wisdom of Proverbs now? Matt. 6:20 **But lay up for yourselves treasures in heaven, where neither moth nor rust doth corrupt, and where thieves do not break through nor steal: 21 For where your treasure is, there will your heart be also.**

What happened to the polished chrome shine, leather adjustable seats, fast glass, and the air-conditioned dream rides that were the answer to all that could be desired? The novelty wore off, as it always does, with any of the many idols that find their way into our hearts. Whether the wants are vacations, dream homes, careers or anything that has replaced the Lord on the throne of our hearts, there will be a disappointment.

The British songwriter Mick Jagger said it best; "I can't get no satisfaction." James 4:2 **Ye lust, and have not: ye kill, and desire to have,** and cannot obtain: ye fight and war, yet ye have not, because ye ask not. 3 **Ye ask, and receive not, because ye ask amiss, that ye may consume it upon your lusts.** There is nothing wrong with asking, but make sure you are asking within your life lived in the Kingdom of God.

Eve has been described as the woman who had everything. Gen. 1:28 **And God blessed them, and God said unto them, Be fruitful, and multiply, and replenish the earth, and subdue it: and have dominion over the fish of the sea, and over the fowl of the air, and over every living thing that moves upon the earth.** What more could a person want? The entire world was given to Adam and his wife Eve.

They were the stewards of everything new and created. What more could be desired? What more could a woman or a man want? The only thing outside of their grasp was the fruit of the one and only tree of knowledge of good and evil. We all know what happened and it begs the question, "Is that the result of getting all that may be desired?"

No matter how much we have, even if it is the entire earth, we will still want more. If Christ is not in control of our hearts, it seems our existence cannot be satisfied. Mark 8:36 **For**

what shall it profit a man, if he shall gain the whole world, and lose his own soul? Is that why God says to run after wisdom, rather than stuff? With wisdom, we will be able to handle all our stuff. Without wisdom, the stuff will own and handle us.

God's wisdom in any situation will be a blessing to our lives and the answer to whatever we are looking for. We can count on the fact that the wisdom God gives us to enjoy with great favor, will promote real life within us. If we choose the Lord's wisdom to work in our lives, it will help us make right what is wrong, make straight what is crooked, and be a blessing to the Kingdom of God.

We will be influencing this world that needs the miraculous love and workings of God. Prov. 2:10 **When wisdom enters into thine heart, and knowledge is pleasant unto thy soul; 11 Discretion shall preserve thee, understanding shall keep thee.** Imagine, God's wisdom is worth far above all that can be desired. Give us this wisdom, Lord, that we may be complete in your love. Amen and amen!

INFINITE AND ETERNAL

Proverbs 29:14 The king that faithfully judges the poor, his throne shall be established for ever.

How can you believe in a God you cannot see? This question is thrown at many believers in Christ and voiced with exasperation on many occasions. Most often after a terrible tragedy caused by human provocation. These people judge God on the actions of a few sick and insane human beings. They want these people controlled by God while demanding their own free will outside of anything God wants for their own lives. They seem to have blinders on and a disconnected understanding of God, whether by choice or spiritual influence. 2Cor. 4:4 **The god of this age has blinded the minds of unbelievers so they cannot see the light of the gospel of the glory of Christ, who is the image of God.**

If God is so good, why do these things go on? This is another empty question that cannot be answered when there is no honest heart to receive what God would express if people were sincere. So they say things like, "Since God will not answer this question to my satisfaction, I am cutting God out of my life." If you are saying things like that, then you have already cut God out a long time before your empty threats were proclaimed.

You might have cut God out of your life but God has not cut you out of His life or plan. There is always hope for the lost and rebellious on this side of the grave. Rom. 5:8 **But God demonstrates his own love for us in this: While we were still sinners, Christ died for us.** What makes it so possible for us believers in Christ to trust the word of the Lord? Why can we trust God absolutely? Num. 23:19 **God is not a man who lies, or a son of man who changes His mind. Does He speak and not act, or promise and not fulfill?**

God is not an eternal man or angel. God is infinite. Angels and all humans are eternal beings because they were created at some point in time. We have a beginning but no end. God is infinite and therefore omnipotent, omnipresent, and omniscient. Throughout eternity we will always be in awe of God because we are only eternal beings while God has always been and will always be infinite.

We have a hard time wrapping our minds around the fact that God always was, is, and will be. Therefore, God had no beginning. God describes Himself as, "I Am." Ex. 3:14 **God said to Moses, "I AM WHO I AM. This is what you are to say to the Israelites: 'I AM has sent me to you.'"** The amazing thing is that God from eternity past was and has always been love and His intention toward us is and has always been love as well. Eph. 1:4 **For He chose us in Christ before the foundation of the world that we may be holy and unblemished in his sight in love.**

The capacity of our infinite God will always be beyond that which we can think or ask even throughout eternity. We will never be infinitely omnipotent, omnipresent, or omniscient like God is. We will always be learning and growing in the unlimited love and power of the Lord. That is why we can trust His leading and love toward us. Our infinite God has chosen us to be His own and has made a way for us to be eternally with Him through Christ Jesus.

There will always be more of our infinite God to know. Whether a billion years as we know time or trillions of decades, God will always be fresh to our eternal lives. Paul, who wrote much of the New Testament, had incredible insight and revelation knowledge as to who the Godhead was and yet, he still wanted to know more. Phil. 3:10

My goal is to know Him and the power of His resurrection and the fellowship of His sufferings, being conformed to His death. Paul could not get enough of God no matter how much he grew in Him, even after deep spiritual experiences, Paul wanted more. 2Cor. 12:2 **I know a man in Christ who fourteen years ago was caught up to the third heaven. Whether it was in the body or out of it I do not know, but God knows.** The more we know Him the more we want Him and His loving grace. Imagine when we are in eternity with Him and we see His glory. We will always be attracted to His infinite love. The purity of His love will envelop us to incredible heights. Rom. 8:18 **For I consider that the sufferings of this present time are not worthy to be compared with the glory that is to be revealed to us.**

Before we judge God as to how He runs things, remember He is doing it from a position of infinite insight. As hard as this is for some humans to hear, we do not know what God knows except through His word. Most of the world doesn't even have one of the Lord's teachings working in their lives, as in, "Love thy neighbour as thy self." Then these same people presume to know how God should run things.

Self-righteousness will do that and cause that type of thinking. Self-righteousness will cause a created eternal being to sit back and judge an infinite loving God and declare what God should do. Isa. 14:13 **You said in your heart, 'I'll ascend to heaven, above the stars of God. I'll erect my throne; I'll sit on the Mount of Assembly in the far reaches of the north;** 14 **I'll ascend above the tops of the clouds; I'll make myself like the Most High.'**

The last time a created being said he would come against God, he came crashing down and lost his position and authority. Eze. 28:18 **By the multitude of your iniquities, through the sinfulness of your trade, you desecrated your sanctuaries. So I drew fire out from within you; it consumed you, and I turned you to ashes on the earth before the eyes of all who saw you.** We are so blessed to have been given eternal life through a loving infinite God. It is the infinite power of God's love that sustains us as eternal beings. Psalm 147:5 **Great is our Lord, and of great power: His understanding is infinite.** Praise the Lord!

FOR BETTER OR WORSE

Proverbs 27:5 Better an open reprimand than concealed love.

For better, of course. Why would we choose worse? Well, it seems this question is not as simple to answer as it sounds. People are choosing worse on a regular basis. They choose the worst parts of the human condition; theft, abuse, genocide and a basket full of other griefs every day. As for me and my house, I choose better. A better covenant, a better way, a better life, and a better relationship with my Lord.

Better is better all around. As known by many in the faith, Jesus did not come to die on the cross to make bad people good. Jesus was crucified to make dead people live through the righteousness of Jesus Christ, and that is a better covenant. The Lord's covenant is better than trying to balance bad acts, thoughts, and behaviors with good ones.

The Lord's covenant is a righteous blessing that gives eternal life to all who accept it by faith in Jesus Christ. Heb. 7:22 **Because of this oath, Jesus has become the guarantor of a**

better covenant. Therefore, having such a better covenant working on our behalf we would be fools not to enter into it with a full heart of expectation toward God and the joy of the Lord in our souls. Heb. 8:6 **But now hath He obtained a more excellent ministry, by how much also He is the mediator of a better covenant, which was established upon better promises.**

When God leads us into righteousness, He often does it with a correction to our character so that we take on the character of Christ. Prov.27:5a **Better an open reprimand.** Someone might say how is being reprimanded a better thing? If I am corrected before I fall on my face, then I welcome the correction and move on to better things. The underlying value of this correction also proves the love God has for me because He corrects those He loves. Prov. 3:11 **My son, do not reject the LORD's discipline, and do not despise his correction.**

Choosing a vibrant relationship with God and man is not always easy but it is always wise. Would there be less war in the world if better choices had been made before the war erupted? Of course, there would be more peace in the world if choices were made from a position of being a blessing rather than a position of taking all you can get at any cost.

Would there be less divorce in society if love and respect was chosen during the hard times? Yes, you know it would have gone better for both people if they had just chosen a better way to express love to each other rather than make it all about me! I realize there are impossible situations in the world and in life which will result in war, divorce, and conflict but why should you be the reason for that mess? Fix the war and conflict within your own soul and reach out and bring the balm of healing to the rest of the world.

Paul, who wrote so much of the New Testament, was before his conversion to Christ a religious zealot. Saul of Tarsus, as he was known then, was putting Christians to death. Acts 9:1 **And Saul, yet breathing out threatenings and slaughter against the disciples of the Lord, went unto the high priest.** After meeting God on his way to Damascus, Paul received the correction, reprimand, and direction of the Lord. At that point, Paul chose a better way to live. He was once the persecutor and became the persecuted because of his better choice, but oh, what a blessing he became to the Christian faith. He helped us all understand the new birth in Christ in a better and righteous way.

So many of our choices in life are for better

or worse. We might be living with the result of the worse choice we made in the past. We might feel like there is no way out of the terrible choice we selfishly went with and we are in the worst situation possible. Take heart saints, Jesus is still Lord over all the earth and He can and will help us if we let Him. He says you are better than the mess you are in and worth more. Matt. 6:26 **Behold the fowls of the air: for they sow not, neither do they reap, nor gather into barns; yet your heavenly Father feeds them. Are ye not much better than they?**

Christ knows the value your heavenly Father has for you. Jesus gave himself for us all at the cross so that we would have the faith and ability to make better choices in this fallen world. We can be assured of the Lord's victory because He says He has overcome this world. John 16:33 **I have told you these things, so that in me you may have peace. In this world you will have trouble. But take heart! I have overcome the world.** For better or worse is put before us daily. Choose better because it is life and it is a better life of salvation. Amen.

EVEN FAITH HEALERS DIE

Proverbs 14:27 The fear of the LORD is a fountain of life, to depart from the snares of death.

1Corinthians 15:26 **The last enemy that shall be destroyed is death.**

I know this is going to come across as bothersome to North Americans, but we will all be inconvenienced with dying one day. This "I want it all" generation thinks they will be in control to the end; however, there is one who has the say as to the number of our days on this earth. Job 14:5 **A man's days are numbered. You know the number of his months. He cannot live longer than the time You have set.** This is why we are admonished to live and enjoy the day we are in today. Psalm 118:24 **This is the day which the LORD hath made; we will rejoice and be glad in it.** Enjoy your life today as it is the only one you have.

The only way out of death's grasp is through the Lord Jesus our Savior. As the proverb says - death is a snare, and that is what every person who has ever lived and is now living tries to escape from. Escaping the snare, grasp, or the inevitable clutches of death keeps people in fear of living truly free and assured lives.

We, on our own and of ourselves, cannot defeat this last enemy that mankind must face with our own cunning and bravado. It takes a supernatural God to get us through death's door and come through the other side complete in Christ and manifested into the fullness of our being. Psalm 48:14 **For this God is our God for ever and ever: he will be our guide even unto death.**

Jesus conquered death through His resurrection from the dead. Christ took the power of death's ability to corrupt and destroy the soul of man and gave every man who has received Jesus as Lord the same resurrection power that raised Jesus from the grave. 1Cor. 15:55 **O death, where is thy sting? O grave, where is thy victory?** True, we will all physically die, but no longer in abject terror, as Jesus will be our guide unto and through death.

Yes, even faith healers will die but no longer dreading the corruption, decay and stinging death once reigned from. Jesus secured the keys of death and hell so we would not have to live through it. Rev. 1:18 **I am the living one. I died, but look--I am alive forever and ever! And I**

hold the keys of death and the grave.

Even faith healers, ministers, and all the righteous in Christ do die but thank God Jesus has overcome death on our behalf. This is the good news that we will be with the Lord and death has no ownership on our souls. 2Cor. 5:8 **In fact, we are confident, and we would prefer to be away from the body and at home with the Lord.**

Someone might say that I may sound a bit morbid talking about death as if it was some kind of thing to look forward to. Not so. I am happy to be living a full and virtuous life and am able to do so because death has been defeated on my behalf. I can be at peace and do what the Lord has put on my heart because the fear of eternal death has no more reach into my existence.

We have been bought and paid for in full by the blood of Christ and the finished work of the cross Jesus was nailed to. Our sins and judgment were nailed to the cross the day we accepted Jesus as Lord. I personally have no desire to go back and give myself over to the snares of death and all its tortures.

I look to the One who has given me all of His righteousness and grace and I feed my heart and life on that wonderful gift of God's love. When I die, it will be with and in the Lord my God.

Death, the last enemy, has been defeated by my Lord and Savior. What an amazing love God has for us. 1Cor. 15:26 **The last enemy that shall be destroyed is death.** Blessings.

LAST WORDS

Proverbs 1:23 Turn you at my reproof: behold, I will pour out my spirit unto you, I will make known my words unto you.

"Make sure your words are sweet because you might have to eat them one day." John Osteen.

I was talking with my son this week and he was feeling sad for one of his friends who had just lost their father in a car accident and his friend was going over the last words that had been spoken between them. My son thanked me for teaching him to make sure our departing words were always kind and full of love. Prov. 16:24 **Pleasant words are honey from a honeycomb — sweet to the soul and healing for the body.**

This lesson was made real to me one afternoon at work when one of the managers I knew within the building I worked from was going out to lunch and I said to him, "See you later," and he jokingly said, "Not if I see you first." I smiled and said "Love you man" in that hardy har type of voice. This conversation was ordinary and even flippant and not much thought was taken to the things said until I found out later that day that he had died at lunchtime of a heart attack. His last words to me no longer mattered because he was no longer here, but my last words did matter because I had to live with them and I was grateful that my last words had been, "Love you man." Even though they had been said in jest, they were my last words nonetheless.

How many husbands and wives wish they could take back some of the hurtful, selfish, or mean words that were said in order to wound the other's heart and soul? How many last words to parents or siblings should not have been uttered because of the life lasting bruises they created? Prov. 18:21 **The tongue has the power of life and death, and those who love it will eat its fruit.**

There is a reason why God admonishes us to make sure we are not going to bed with anger and angry words in our heart toward our spouse. Don't go to bed angry with words of death ready to bust out at the slightest provocation. Eph. 4:26 **And "don't sin by letting anger control you." Don't let the sun go down while you are still angry,** 27 **for anger gives a foothold to the devil.** What if your spouse were to pass away during the night? Would the rest of your life be haunted with a twinge of guilt that the devil could bring up regularly to accuse you?

Was the last sound that came from your teenager a slamming door and a barrage of acrimonious slander toward God and man? After years of no communication over a stupid argument, how many parents would now put up with a tattoo or two and a ring here and there just to have their son back in right standing with the family? No, saints, these are not happy thoughts. These things are going on all over and all the time. The Lord is the only one with the right answer for these sad cases. Psalm 19:14 **Let the words of my mouth, and the meditation of my heart, be acceptable in thy sight, O LORD, my strength, and my redeemer.**

I know there are varying reasons for all the mayhem in families and friendships gone bad these days, but how much of the shrapnel flying about is the result of the last words said to one another? Maybe if we had tucked our pride away - just for a moment - and not spewed the hurting words, we would be living happier lives. Instead of spending the majority of our lives trying to repair broken relationships, we would actually be fulfilled because of loving relationships.

I will paraphrase the prodigal son's last words to his father. "Give me my money and get out of the way, I'm going to do it my way." Luke

15:16 The younger of them said to his father, 'Father, give me the share of the estate I have coming to me.' So he distributed the assets to them.

We all know the story of how this brat came to himself when he was coveting the pig food the pigs were eating. The son said (paraphrased), "I've messed up royally, and I need to go home and apologize to my father who has always been good and fair to me." Luke 15:18 **I will set out and go back to my father and say to him: Father, I have sinned against heaven and against you.**

Why was he able to go back? Because his father had not used the self-righteousness card when he had the right and the chance to do it. The father had remained a loving father who kept his last words sweet toward his son who was shaming him publicly. What courage and fortitude it took for the father to see his son through the eyes of God. We too are so fortunate to have a loving heavenly Father with kind words for us.

At the end of the day, are our last words to God the Father sometimes stout and arrogant? I hope not. God's thoughts and words toward us are words of love and encouragement. Jer. 29:11 **For I know the plans I have for you," declares the LORD, "plans to prosper you and not to harm you, plans to give you hope and a future.**

Maybe it is time to pick up the phone, write, email or face time that family member who is estranged because of poorly chosen words in the heat of the argument. Maybe it is time to be righteous, rather than right.

I know you can do it because Jesus' last words were a promise of power that would come from the Holy Spirit upon us to do what it will take to get the love of God filling the earth. So, I know you can call those who are hurt and make your words as sweet as the love of God so they will come home. Acts 1:8 **But you will receive power when the Holy Spirit has come on you, and you will be My witnesses in Jerusalem, in all Judea and Samaria, and to the ends of the earth.**

Yes, stop watering dead plants, but make sure you water what the Holy Spirit says to nurture, protect, and love back into fellowship, so that the Lord can heal us all. Amen and amen!

PART FIVE:

QUESTIONS FOR UNDERSTANDING

1. *What did you learn in this section of the book?*
2. *What surprised you the most?*
3. *What subject(s) spoke to your heart?*
4. *Did the material that you read help you understand the subject(s) more or less?*
5. *What topics are important to you? Why?*
6. *How do these articles relate to you?*
7. *After reading this section of the book, what will you change in your life?*

ABOUT THE AUTHOR

I have been in Christian ministry in one form or another for over forty years. In 1980 I attended Commonwealth Bible College in Katoomba, New South Wales, Australia.

At that time I was involved in prison ministries, preaching on the radio in a small town, and church-related works of all kinds. I have taught bible college courses and also have been involved in personal discipleship training. God has blessed me all along the way. Now I have the opportunity to write down what was experienced throughout the years. The Lord has blessed me with sound and forthright material to write a series of Christian devotionals. I have lived the testimonies on these pages and can attest to the fact that God is so faithful and good. My hope is that your soul will be enriched as you read this book. God bless you.

CONNECT WITH NORM

Norm's Blog "Sir Norm's Proverbial Comment" can be found online in English, French and Spanish. Your comments on any of the hundreds of blog posts are appreciated.

www.sirnorm.com

www.ingramcontent.com/pod-product-compliance
Lightning Source LLC
Chambersburg PA
CBHW070345090426
42733CB00009B/1297